THE ADVENTUROUS GARDENER'S SOURCEBOOK OF RARE AND UNUSUAL PLANTS

William C. Mulligan

PHOTOGRAPHY BY
Elvin McDonald

SIMON & SCHUSTER

NEW YORK LONDON TORONTO SYDNEY
TOKYO SINGAPORE

for Philip Muth

A RUNNING HEADS BOOK
Copyright © 1992 by Running Heads Incorporated

SIMON & SCHUSTER
Simon & Schuster Building
Rockefeller Center
1230 Avenue of the Americas
New York, N.Y. 10020
SIMON & SCHUSTER and colophon are registered trademarks
of Simon & Schuster Inc.

THE ADVENTUROUS GARDENER'S SOURCEBOOK OF
RARE AND UNUSUAL PLANTS
was conceived and produced by
Running Heads Incorporated
55 West 21 Street
New York, N.Y. 10010

Creative Director: Linda Winters
Editor: Rose K. Phillips
Designer: Jan Melchior
Managing Editor: Jill Hamilton
Production Associate: Belinda Hellinger
10 9 8 7 6 5 4 3 2 1

Library of Congress Cataloging-in-Publication Data
Mulligan, William C., 1942–
The adventurous gardener's sourcebook of rare and unusual plants /
William C. Mulligan ; photography by Elvin McDonald.
p.   cm.
"A Running Heads book" — T.p. verso.
Includes bibliographical references and index.
ISBN 0-671-75104-2
1. Rare garden plants.   2. Plants, Cultivated.   I. Title.
SB454.3.R37M86   1992
635.9 — dc20   92-12060
CIP

Typeset by Trufont Typographers Inc.
Color separations by Hong Kong Scanner Craft Company, Ltd.
Printed and bound in Singapore by Tien Wah Press (Pte.) Ltd.

Acknowledgments

Thanks especially to all the gardeners who shared generously of themselves and permitted us to photograph: Jean Atwater, Ernesta Drinker Ballard, David Barnett, William Barrick, Jr., Judy Becker, Berry Botanic Garden, Kim Bodger, Robert Bowden, John Brookes, John Buchanan, Albert and Diantha Buell, Caroline Burgess, Coleman and Susan Burke, Butchart Gardens, Frank Cabot, Brandon and Emily Chenault, Mabel Corwin, Rosalind Creasy, Fiona Crumley, Bernard Currid, Lea Davies, Robert de Laney, Thomas Henry Dodd, Jr., Douglas Dudgeon, John Elsley, J. Barry Ferguson, Robert Florence, Steven Frowine, William Giambalvo, Betty Graubaum, Dave Grigsby, C.Z. Guest, Marilyn Hampstead, John M. Harris, Robert Hayes, Howard Irwin, Karen Park Jennings, Ron Johnson, Gordon Jones, Michael Kartuz, Lamb Nurseries, Robert Lilly, Christopher Lloyd, Longwood Gardens, Ann Lovejoy, Bonny and David Martin, Joy Logee Martin, Tovah Martin, Jean Merkel, Everitt Miller, Lynden B. Miller, Victor Nelson, Peter K. Nelson, Robert Newgarden, Ellen and Shepherd Ogden, J. Liddon Pennock, Jr., Kathy and Duncan Pitney, Lawrence V. Power, Ghilean Prance, Michael Ramirez, Sarah Price, Sally Reath, Mary Ringer, Frank Robinson, Virginia Robinson Gardens, Michael Ruggiero, Daniel Ryniec, Stephen Scanniello, George Schoellkopf, Elizabeth Scholtz, Jerry Sedenko, Peter Selig, Ellie and Joel Spingarn, Timothy Steinhoff, Nelson Sterner, David Tarrant, Kent Taylor, Sir John Thouron, Nikki Threlkeld, Joyce Van Etten, Rosemary Verey, Phillip Watson, Ira Walker, Katherine Whiteside, John Whitworth, Jr., Patrick Worley, Louise Wrinkle, Linda Yang and Barry Yinger. We appreciate also the professionalism and enthusiastic contribution of the home team at Running Heads: Rose K. Phillips, Anne Halpin, Jill Hamilton, Jan Melchior, and Linda Winters. 🦎

William C. Mulligan, Author

Elvin McDonald, Photographer

CONTENTS

INTRODUCTION

The day I resolved to write this book I was serendipitously invited to the monthly dinner and forum of the Hortus Club of New York. Hortus means simply "garden," suggesting enclosure, and the members of this group have an all-consuming love of plants. Many are professionals whose livelihoods are intertwined with the botanical world. Others are passionate amateurs. At meetings, they share stories and color slides of extraordinary individual plants and their habitats, both wild and cultivated. They also arrive at every meeting hoping to stump each other with a specimen no one can identify. It is unlikely that this could ever occur, since these are individuals who are so plant-literate that they needn't even inspect any given plant closely to ascertain its identity — and yet, these passionate plants people continue to challenge each other. The program for that particular evening was koten engei or Japanese classical plant culture — virtually unexplored territory even for these experts. The speaker, Barry Yinger, has traveled to Japan more than twenty times on plant-hunting expeditions. The practice of koten engei is ancient, even predating bonsai. It entails using earthenware pots to grow such common plants as rohdea (Rohdea) and wild ginger (Asarum), but only extremely rare, even one-of-a-kind, varieties. These are regularly entered in competitions dictated by rules and customs that have evolved over hundreds of years, a ritual practiced almost entirely by males. Such wild ginger species as A. canadense and A. europaeum are widely distributed over the Northern Hemisphere, so much so that many variations can be recognized. The entries in koten engei competitions are judged on such minutiae as whether the leaf lobes meet or overlap slightly. Such variation can make a big difference in a plant's appraised value: According to annual rating charts listing a multitude of Asarum varieties and their worth, the plant having a "perfect" leaf could be valued at a quarter of a million dollars, while one with gaping lobes and plain color might command a modest sum of $2.50. Intrigued, I paid a visit to Yinger's domain in Far Hills, New Jersey, where he

PLANTSMAN BARRY YINGER HOLDS RARE *ASARUM*, OBTAINED IN JAPAN FROM A PRACTITIONER OF *KOTEN ENGEI*, OR JAPANESE CLASSICAL PLANT CULTURE. *ASARUM CANADENSE* (opposite) DISPLAYS THE HIGHLY DESIRABLE TRAIT OF LOBES THAT MEET OR OVERLAP SLIGHTLY. (Previous pages) MUSHROOMS AND OTHER FUNGI REPRESENT A VAST KINGDOM OF LITTLE-KNOWN PLANTS.

acts as director of the Leonard J. Buck Gardens. There, in his collection of gingers, I saw the essence of koten engei. Liberty Hyde Bailey, that titan of the plant world, described just such an intense collection in his 1928 book, The Garden Lover: "He admires his plants alone when nobody is looking, and loves to be with them for companionship in all odd hours. . . . When not in bloom they are his, at morning, noon and night. With discernment and discrimination he talks about them now and then with sympathetic friends." Recognizing this universal trait among gardeners to cultivate personal relationships with their plants, I decided to seek out others with Yinger's adventurous and dauntless spirit. I journeyed to Semmes, Alabama, to visit Thomas Henry Dodd, Jr., a nurseryman who specializes in woody plants and has recently been honored by the American Horticultural Society for his persistence and generosity in disseminating plants meriting more attention. In an industry that has for most of this century followed a trend of growing more and more of less and less, Dodd has stood up for diversity. With Yinger and others he has embarked on noteworthy plant-exploration journeys in search of unusual native American flora that could be adapted to commercial production. He also has an intense interest in non-natives. Indeed, one of the most outstanding plants in his collection, grown from seeds Yinger collected in China, is a species of Petunia covered with glowing rose-magenta flowers in spring. The magnificent specimens that these gardeners cultivate are among the visual delights in these pages. I continued my plant quest in England. Photographer Elvin McDonald and I were invited to tour the private gardens of a rather famous couple of commerce and industry. Since we were guests of the head gardener and not the owners, all cameras were left locked in the car, so this is one story for which the reader must take my word: There in the middle of a bed filled with annual and perennial treasures was a breathtaking purple-leaved ornamental whose label proclaimed it to be Plantago major 'Atropurpurea.' Without the descriptive Latin 'Atropurpurea' (dark purple) this botanical name simply indicates Plantago major, or plantain, a plain green weed that inhabits about as many lawns around the world as the dandelion. Even as we were admiring 'Atropurpurea' the gardener pointed out that I was standing on a green one — that is, a "weed" — in the lawn. By the by, another species in the same genus, P. psyllium, from the eastern Mediterranean region, naturalized in eastern North America, is the source of psyllium-husk fiber. Little-known or obscure facts like this titillate the adventurous gardener, whose need is not so much to have something that others don't, but rather to step outside the everyday. THE ADVEN-TUROUS GARDENER'S SOURCEBOOK OF RARE AND UNUSUAL PLANTS is filled with plants that seem to

SEEDS FOR THIS COLD-, HEAT-, AND DROUGHT-TOLERANT PETUNIA SPECIES,
SEEN BLOOMING IN EARLY SPRING, WERE BROUGHT FROM
CHINA TO ALABAMA NURSERYMAN TOM DODD BY A FELLOW PLANT EXPLORER.

have been waiting in the wings for decades, maybe centuries. By not being part of the everyday plant palette, they have acquired a cachet that makes them especially appealing. Growing and collecting them is not driven by a mainstream sensibility but by an appreciation of their beauty, rarity relative to other plants, and intriguing histories. By only pursuing esoteric species is the adventurous gardener a snob? Not at all. Just curious, opinionated, and appreciative of details. The word "adventurous" can have connotations of daring, and, in a sense, the adventurous gardener dares to be different, cultivating rare or little-known plants that seem destined to be appreciated by a chosen few, an inner sanctum of disciples or initiates. Some of us can learn about plants, some will never have any interest, and others will always seem to know and appreciate all flora, from the humble fungi that take up residence on the forest floor to the most towering and magnificent of trees. ✑ There is, of course, a certain risk involved in revealing or touting a little-known plant. If it becomes widely available, it could lose its esoteric appeal and become devalued. But oftentimes outstanding yet little-cultivated plants are not kept under wraps, yet remain rare. The Gold Lace primroses that grace a sunny bed in one of the outdoor rooms at Sissinghurst Castle in England, were planted there originally in the 1940s by the famous writers Vita Sackville-West and Harold Nicolson. A precise gold band edges every petal of these polyanthus-style flowers. Surely untold numbers of the world's most devoted gardeners have visited Sissinghurst every May while the Gold Laces are out. Wouldn't they naturally covet seeds or plants? Why then doesn't the Gold Lace primula become common? Dr. Bailey might just have the answer

when, in The Garden Lover he explains: ". . . many plant-growers would not sell a plant, but they would give away an armful of roots; the plants are too good to be sold." Apparently the "undiscovered" plant has not only a mysterious aura, it also possesses more inherent virtue than those found at every nursery and in neighbors' gardens. ⟨⟩ The purpose of this volume is to acquaint readers with the remarkable possibilities. Adventurous gardeners can use the temperature ranges or U.S.D.A. plant hardiness zones, referring to the map on page 224, to determine which plants are most likely to flourish in their home environment.

AT SISSINGHURST CASTLE GARDENS,
IN KENT, ENGLAND, GOLD LACE PRIMROSES
APPEAR IN MAY AS THEY HAVE EVERY SPRING
SINCE PLANTED BY VITA SACKVILLE-WEST
AND HAROLD NICOLSON IN THE 1940S.

Armed with this information, they can knowledgeably peruse plant catalogues, make special requests from nurseries, and even join specialty plant societies that will allow them to focus their attention on particular species. In a sense, they can act as modern-day plant hunters — without having to embark on long, arduous journeys — as they have centuries' worth of plants at their fingertips. Individuals with a bent for horticulture will take extreme pleasure in observing all the differences in plants, while those with an appreciation for botanical taxonomy will seek out the similarities. Either way, an abundant selection and treasure trove await gardeners with a love of adventure.

CHAPTER
ONE

PRIZED
PERENNIALS

There are few things that are quite so thrilling to a gardener as being a part of the yearly cycle of a perennial flower, which returns to the ground each year only to re-emerge the next in a riot of bloom. After dark winter months, to see sprouts emerging from the nurturing earth in spring is cause for celebration. The process is akin to old friends reuniting after a long separation. ❧ Not since the age of the renowned British artist and gardener Gertrude Jekyll — nearly a century ago — have gardeners shown such passion for perennial plantings. Jekyll's favorites, such as delphinium, foxglove, and summer phlox, still reign in the mind's eye as essential garden ingredients, along with such complementary plants as herbaceous peony, German and Siberian irises, daylily, hosta, chrysanthemum, and aster. Among these classics, what is there to spark the imagination and taste for the unusual? Not to worry, in the scheme of things horticultural there is an endless supply of plants that remain just elusive enough to make them highly desirable. All of this is relative, of course, to one's specific experience and sense of appreciable difference. The beginner who has not yet befriended astilbe might well fall in love with the plant, yet the seasoned gardener understands that this exceptional plant is not at all unusual and is merely one of the bread-and-butter staples. The solid yellow and short-stemmed cultivar of Belamcanda chinensis illustrated in these pages is more to the point of this chapter. Generosity with seeds and quickness to regenerate have made the belamcanda, or blackberry lily, as it is more adventurously called, a favorite of the cottage gardeners of the world, but not of much interest to the commercial grower, who must offer plants that are not so self-reliant. Folk plants, those that are mostly given away or bartered from gardener to gardener, are by nature mysteriously appealing, for their origins lie not in well-labelled nursery beds, but in the distant past, traded by gardeners through the generations. Belamcanda is ordinarily orange with red spots, so a solid yellow specimen becomes the crème de la crème of the unusual.

❧ After reading this chapter, the reader may well wonder which plants for one reason or another got away but beg mentioning. At the top of the list are Dicentra pusilla, a tiny bleeding heart from Japan, Artemisia 'Powis Castle,' which is taller and less lacy than 'Silver Mound,' yet shorter, more refined, and better smelling than 'Silver Queen' and 'Silver King'; 'Baby Lucia' pansy, a true miniature that self-sows delightfully; and Nepeta govaniana, a vigorous plant from Kashmir, easily grown from seed to three feet high and displaying abundant pale-yellow flowers in July. All of these plants are worth seeking out and would certainly receive their own entries if space allowed. The species that follow each have considerable merit and certainly deserve a place in the perennial gardens of the adventurous.

BELAMCANDA CHINENSIS (previous two pages) BLOOMS IN THE PENNSYLVANIA GARDEN OF SIR JOHN THOURON. A BLUE ACCENT IS PROVIDED BY ECHIUM VULGARE 'BLUE BEDDER.' THE GERANIUM 'JOHNSON'S BLUE' (opposite) GROWS IN THE CONNECTICUT GARDEN OF GEORGE SCHOELLKOPF AND RON JOHNSON.

ACONITUM ANTHORA

Gardeners are inclined to pigeonhole the monkshoods as something poisonous, and to take or leave them as something tall and blue for the autumn garden. This is a pity, for there are numerous purples, blues, whites, and bicolor blues-and-whites among the clan. The flowering season begins after the longest day, in midsummer. *Aconitum carmichaelii wilsonii* is one of the tallest monkshoods, growing to six feet and more, and blooming from September to October. To keep the tall stems erect, staking is suggested.

Perhaps the biggest surprise comes with the yellow and pink monkshoods, a fact that could seem amusing to a non-gardener but is good news if one is needing just this sort of hardy perennial. The rare *A. anthora* has creamy yellow flowers, each including the requisite hemispheric helmet-shaped blossoms. These appear from July to August on a sturdy plant growing 20 to 24 inches tall. Lamb Nurseries of Spokane, Washington, where the accompanying photograph was taken, also cultivates *A. napellus* 'Carneum' or *A. compactum*, promising a delicate pink bloom, also in June through August.

Monkshoods in general have finely cut leaves similar to those of delphiniums. They are hardy-to-well below 0°F. but protracted hot weather is not to their liking. Give them sun to partial shade in a humus-rich, well-drained, moist soil. They make a superb display of cut flowers.

ACONITUM ANTHORA (opposite) IS A RARE, CREAMY YELLOW MONKSHOOD FOR MID-TO LATE SUMMER. *ARUNCUS DIOICUS* (right) IS A CLOUD OF IVORY PLUMES GROWING TO A TOWERING SEVEN FEET ABOVE INTENSE GREEN FOLIAGE IN SUMMER.

ARUNCUS DIOICUS

Goatsbeard may be the common name for *Aruncus dioicus*, but its feathery, creamy white plumes are more likely to remind you of astilbe flowers. (However, the two are not related; the genus *Aruncus* belongs to the Rose Family, while *Astilbe* is a member of the Saxifrages.) This commanding plant grows five to seven feet tall. As to its needs, take a clue from its native habitat: rich, moist woodland of North America, Europe, and

Asia. With ample water and partial shade, large clumps develop. The cultivar 'Child of Two Worlds' ('Zweiweltenkind') grows to four feet and boasts pendulous, ivory white plumes.

There is also a dwarf and highly recommended goatsbeard, *A. aethusifolius*, for sun or shade, that produces a very small mound of finely cut foliage that spreads to a full 12 inches across. Above the leaves are borne four-inch spikes of creamy white flowers in summer. If left to mature rather than dead-headed, the spent seedheads give a bold sculptural effect.

ASTRANTIA MAJOR

Astrantia is one of those plants whose fine qualities seedsmen wish they could get their customers to appreciate. Perhaps what they see in this member of the carrot family is that, in the right place, it is one of summer's loveliest flowers, in the garden or in bouquets. *Astrantia major*, from the Caucasus, is a hardy perennial that is well behaved, stands two feet tall and spreads about as broad, giving a lacy, sprightly effect all summer until frost. It grows best in a partially shaded area where there is a dependable supply of moisture. The plant has basal, palmate leaves like those of hardy geranium and almost daisy-like flowers on sparsely branched, naked scapes. The color of these can vary from pink to white to greenish, the colors occurring sometimes individually, other times in one flower.

An ideal site is partly shady in summer, near a stream, in deep, woodsy soil. If timing is everything, then maybe that is astrantia's strong point. Its starry flowers follow the abundance of spring blooms — columbines, foamflowers, and the like — and it makes a wonderful companion plant to grow alongside old-fashioned cottage garden pinks, behind the coralbells, and around the shrub roses. It is also flattering to *Nepeta mussinii*.

Part of the seedsman's dilemma is that while astrantia is an exciting plant to offer, once established, it self-sows. Adventurous gardeners, by and large generous souls, are all too eager to assist gardening friends in transplanting some of their excess. If seeds are proffered, take them and plant at once in a cold frame or other protected place outdoors. The fresher astrantia's just-ripened seeds, the better they will germinate.

ASTRANTIA MAJOR, OR MASTERWORT, IS A MEMBER
OF THE CARROT FAMILY, WITH ONE-INCH,
CREAMY WHITE FLOWER DOMES SURROUNDED BY
A RUFF OF GREENISH WHITE BRACTS.

AUBRIETA 'BORSCH'S WHITE'

One way for a plant to enter the realm of esoterica is to exist in a color not generally found in its genus. *Aubrieta* 'Borsch's White' is just that, the only white in a crowd of blue, purple, and red rock cresses. It has another distinction, possibly dubious, shared with the other aubrietas: They prefer life in England, the Pacific Northwest, or any place that is *not* hot and dry in summer. But no matter the postal code, the gardener who loves a challenge will provide full sun and perfect drainage and propagate new stock from cuttings every spring as flowering finishes. There is, by the way, confusion about the name of rock cress. *Aubrieta* (aw-bree-tuh) is the official pronunciation; but aubretia (aw-bree-shuh) is commonly heard. Those with a serious interest will opt for the former.

COREOPSIS ROSEA

My favorite gardening encyclopedia has a page of fine print devoted to *Coreopsis* alone, all described yellow, orange, or mahogany red — save one. Yes, there is a rose coreopsis, *C. rosea*, which is native to eastern North America. Though a wildflower, this slender-stemmed plant can be coaxed into growing in the home garden, provided it is given a moist soil and ample sun — a meadow-like atmosphere. The rosy pink flowers with their sunny centers bring distinction to floral arrangements, as they are quite long-lasting cut flowers. The plant grows 12 to 18 inches tall, and the flowers are borne amid the deep green, finely divided leaves. Coreopsis are variously annual and perennial. Recent breeding has produced some outstanding cultivars that bloom the first year from seed but are, in fact, hardy perennials.

CRAMBE CORDIFOLIA

Crambe cordifolia is one of the largest herbaceous perennials cultivated in gardens. In full bloom, it creates a midsummer spectacle not soon forgotten. Such boldness also requires space. Otherwise a small yard must be given over to this enormous crucifer, known commonly as the colewort or giant sea kale. Regular sea kale, familiar in some European kitchen gardens, is *C. maritima*; its shoots are blanched in the spring and harvested like culinary asparagus. In her must-read book *The Border in Bloom*, Ann Lovejoy suggests *C. cordifolia* for altering a not entirely pleasant view by scrim effect rather than as a full block-out, for it contributes to "the vital element of mystery so often lacking in our small gardens."

Giant sea kale grows to seven feet tall and as wide, first producing heart-shaped basal leaves to two feet across, then sending up in summer the tall, leafless, branching panicles which bear multitudes of small white, fragrant flowers. Crambe does best in sandy, well-drained, limey soil, with an abundance of sunlight and air. It languishes and may soon die out in sticky or heavy clay. Propagation is by division of the roots at spring planting time or from seeds. The sea kales are true coles, as is kale; "sea" simply refers to their culture in the sandy loams of European beaches and lowlands.

CYNOGLOSSUM GRANDE

Cynoglossum grande is an American native perennial originally from the Pacific Coast. It can grow one to three feet tall, displaying white-eyed blue or purple, forget-me-not-type flowers for summer borders. Remember to divide the roots in spring or autumn. The plant has no quarrel with winter's chill and is hardy to 0°F. or colder in well-drained soil. Summer can present a problem, however, as it suffers in places with hot and dry spells. The common names for this plant, hound's tongue (for the rough-hairy texture of the leaves) and beggar's-lice (for the stick-tight seeds) may not sound pretty, but they are certainly descriptive of this most unusual plant.

CYPRIPEDIUM ACAULE

Cypridpedium acaule, while one of the most difficult lady's-slipper orchid species to introduce into a new area, is a lovely sight in its natural habitat of dry woods. It ranges from Newfoundland to North Carolina and westward to Minnesota. Aside from other-worldly beauty for a few all-too-brief days or weeks in spring, something remarkable about this native orchid is its symbiotic relationship with microrrhizae — highly specialized fungi present in the habitat soil that enable the cypripedium roots to assimilate nutrients, and vice versa. Moccasin-flower, as this species is also known, sends up two large leaves, to eight inches long, from the base. Single flowers, in shades of pink and with the characteristic pouch-like lip, nod gracefully on ten-inch stalks from May through June. It's worth taking the time to meet this discriminating plant's needs: an acid, well-drained, rather dry soil — in which are present the very special "friendly" fungi — and partial shade.

ARTIST AND GARDENER JEAN ATWATER STANDS BESIDE *CRAMBE CORDIFOLIA* (opposite) BLOOMING IN JULY AT HER LOCAL NURSERY, LAMB OF SPOKANE, WASHINGTON.

CRAMBE CORDIFOLIA (above) RESEMBLES AN OVERFED BABY'S-BREATH BUT BELONGS TO THE CRUCIFERS. *CRAMBE MARITIMA* IS THE SEA KALE OF THE FRENCH *POTAGER*.

DELPHINIUM SEMIBARBATUM

This tuberous-rooted perennial from Iran, also known as *Delphinium* 'Zalil', sends up bright yellow flowers in racemes to 30 inches tall in summer. What's unusual about this plant is that delphiniums are ordinarily blue, white, pink, or purple. The scarlet larkspur, *D. cardinale*, which can be found from Baja California north to central California, introduces another unexpected color: scarlet sepals with scarlet-tipped upper petals that are yellow. This species has unusually deep, thick, and woody roots, which are well able to support the erect stems that grow to six feet. The red larkspur, *D. nudicaule*, which ranges from California to southern Oregon, grows to two feet, and has orange-red, brick red, or yellow flowers. And if green flowers are one's specialty, there's *D.* 'Green Expectations'.

DIASCIA RIGESCENS

DIANTHUS KNAPPII

This plant belongs to the genus of the garden pinks, most of which are aptly described by their name. But this one is yellow. Native to Yugoslavia, the 18-inch plants, clad in silvery blue foliage, bear clusters of soft yellow flowers. An exceptionally heavy bloomer, *Dianthus knappii* comes true from seed, and establishes colonies. Very hardy, it tolerates cold, heat, and drought. It is lovely in the garden and great for cutting.

Thanks to the Plant Introduction Scheme at the University of British Columbia Botanical Garden in Vancouver, *Diascia rigescens* is enjoying an unprecedented renaissance. Liberty Hyde Bailey mentioned diascia among the plants he was growing in the 1920s, but this strain originated with a plant received from Windsor Great Park, England, in 1983. It is native to South Africa, needs full sun, has no serious pest or disease problems and is cold hardy to about 0°F. Diascia belongs to the Scrophulariads (snapdragon is also one) and is effective massed in containers or in the ground. It mixes well with blue flowers, such as *Anagallis monelli* 'Pacific Blue', or with warm lavenders such as chive blossoms. Or try Ann Lovejoy's daring combination of its coppery pink with flaming red *Alonsoa warscewiczii*, threading in some of the silvery strands of *Helichrysum petiolare*, that marvelous plant smelling deceptively of licorice when the leaves are gently stroked. *Diascia rigescens* flowers from late spring until frost; regular deadheading improves its appearance.

YELLOW *DELPHINIUM SEMIBARBATUM*, OR *ZALIL*, BLOOMS IN EARLY SUMMER (opposite) AT THE PARK SEED COMPANY IN SOUTH CAROLINA. ROSY PINK *DIASCIA RIGESCENS* (above) WAS RECENTLY INTRODUCED IN NORTH AMERICA.

GAURA LINDHEIMERI

Everywhere I travel I seem to find gaura. In March, along a temporary dirt road within the city of San Antonio, Texas, I came upon *Gaura calcicola*, gray-leaved bushlets hardly a foot tall and smelling sweetly of honeysuckle. In April there was *G. lindheimeri* starting to bloom in a prominent new planting at the Atlanta Botanical Garden. A June visit to Planting Fields Arboretum in Oyster Bay, Long Island, yielded the planting seen here — a second-year clump shining from a mixed herbaceous border, with rambler roses in back and *Achillea* 'Gold Plate' in front. Once more, at the University of British Columbia Botanical Garden in Vancouver, I found my friend *G. lindheimeri*, still flowering in September after an unseasonably hot, dry summer, and sharing a bed with *Ratibida columnifera* and a bronze pennisetum grass.

Gaura lindheimeri is a member of the Evening Primrose Family whose natural range is Louisiana, Texas, and that part of Mexico adjoining Texas. The lance-shaped leaves are downy beneath, maroon-spotted on top. Visionary gardeners have been cultivating lindheimeri for at least a hundred years, but today's Xeriscapers are counting heavily upon gaura, for it tolerates drought. Give it a sunny, well-drained location with enough space for a plant the size of a bushel basket. The vast numbers of white flowers have a charming habit of aging overnight to pink, after which they disappear.

GAURA LINDHEIMERI, OF THE EVENING PRIMROSE
FAMILY, IS IN VOGUE FOR ITS DROUGHT
TOLERANCE, VASE SHAPE, AND GRACEFUL WAND-
LIKE STEMS. BEST OF ALL, ITS MAGICAL WHITE
FLOWERS HOVER LIKE A CLOUD OF SILVERY
MOTHS THAT OVERNIGHT TURN PALE PINK.

GERANIUM MACRORRHIZUM

This true *Geranium*, unlike the tender bedding-plant geranium which belongs to the genus *Pelargonium*, is one of over 300 species of mostly hardy plants widely disbursed over temperate regions and the lower vegetation belt on mountainsides in the tropics. *Geranium macrorrhizum* is a colonizer noteworthy for handsome foliage that is often nearly evergreen, and for the showiness of its flowers. These charm the gardener with a calyx in contrasting color from the petals, and stamens that stretch forth in a most beguiling manner. Numerous garden forms include 'Walter Ingwersen' (soft pink), 'Bevan's Variety' (cerise), and *album* (white). The leaves turn shades of pumpkin, cordovan, and scarlet in autumn, often persisting until spring. A late blue monkshood makes a beautiful partner.

HELLEBORUS FOETIDUS

Christmas and Lenten roses, *Helleborus niger* and *H. orientalis*, are to most gardeners exceptional plants because they bloom in winter and earliest spring when hardly anything herbaceous is flowering. They also have greenish to white, pink, and darkest burgundy flowers that are waxy and quite unlike more familiar blossoms. But more interesting than these is *H. foetidus*, or stinking hellebore, which sounds like it belongs in a witch's cauldron, but which in fact is named for the mildly unpleasant smell given off when its leaves are crushed. The fingery, dark, evergreen leaves are crowned by immense heads carrying hundreds of nodding, purple-edged, pale green flowers, and the plants grow to an overall height of about 18 inches. Bedmates include winter-blooming shrubs such as *Hamamelis* × *intermedia*, *Daphne mezereum*, and *Mahonia japonica*.

THE LEAVES OF *GERANIUM MACRORRHIZUM* (above) COLOR UP IN AUTUMN AND REMAIN UNTIL SUPERSEDED BY NEW GREEN ONES IN SPRING. THE PALE GREEN FLOWERS OF *HELLEBORUS FOETIDUS* (below) ARE TREASURED FOR THEIR WINTER-SPRING BLOOM. LENTEN ROSE, *H. ORIENTALIS* (opposite) ADORNS A STATUE AT DIXON GALLERY AND GARDENS IN MEMPHIS.

HESPERIS MATRONALIS

Ann Lovejoy calls this the sweet rocket of the Elizabethans and describes its flowers as faded greenish white, and similar to phlox. I agree about the phlox part but color is up for grabs: The fragrant blooms may be any color from snow white to dark red-lavender, usually single, rarely double. If sweet rocket is seen blooming in the ideal shade to accompany your favorite German irises and peonies in mid- to late spring, collect its seedpods when they mature (but before they dry up and split open). *Hesperis matronalis* is a member of the Mustard Family that grows from basal leaves to between three and four feet tall at flowering time. The plants grow best as biennials, this summer's seedlings yielding next spring's flowers. But while sweet rocket may be technically a biennial, it self-sows and, once established, the effect is that of a perennial. Sweet rocket is one of the truest folk plants or cottage garden flowers in cultivation, something best gotten from a friend or neighbor; it is rarely seen in catalogues or local nurseries. A stand of sweet rocket in its darker expressions of lavender or red-violet looks beautiful close by flowering chives, *Allium schoenoprasum*, and chartreuse lady's-mantle, *Alchemilla vulgaris*. The pure white form is perfect for an all-white garden and also combines lacily with yellow, blue, and pink flowers. Left on its own, sweet rocket colonizes especially vigorously when part of a nearly wild garden where the soil is humusy and moist.

HESPERIS MATRONALIS (opposite) MIXES WELL WITH COMMON HOP VINE IN LATE SPRING. LYSIMACHIA PUNCTATA (above) BLOOMS LATE SPRING TO SUMMER, L. PROCUMBENS (overleaf, left) MOSTLY DURING SPRING, AND L. CLETHROIDES (overleaf, right) DURING SUMMER.

LYSIMACHIA

Lysimachia, or loosestrife, belongs to the Primrose Family. The genus includes about 165 different annual or perennial herbaceous plants, rarely shrubby, that are widely distributed in temperate and subtropical regions. *Lysimachia punctata*, from Europe, is a tough, hardy perennial that has naturalized in North America. The bright lemon yellow flowers whorl about the three- to four-foot stems throughout June and July. Plant it in full sun or light shade and reasonably moist, well-drained soil.

Lysimachia clethroides, from China and Japan, tightly packs starry, milky white flowers into racemes that all bend over in the same direction, giving rise to the nickname gooseneck. Both of these hardy perennials get on well with daylilies, *Hemerocallis*, or almost any summer flower. Newly introduced to cultivation by Logee's Greenhouses of Connecticut, *L. procumbens* is for mild climate gardens or a sunny window in cold weather. It is a well-behaved trailing plant that bears golden yellow flowers in spring. Hardy golden moneywort, *L. nummularia* 'Aurea', is popular for its foliage color and prostrate habit.

MIMULUS CARDINALIS

Scarlet monkey flower, *Mimulus cardinalis*, is a western American native, its range extending from southern Oregon to northern Mexico, and eastward to Nevada, Utah, and Arizona. It is a freely branching perennial covered with sticky hairs. Its four-foot stems may arch gracefully or stand quite erect. The two-lipped flowers, which grow to about two inches long, vary from scarlet to pale reddish yellow, and have projecting stamens. On a late summer visit to Portland, Oregon, *M. cardinalis* could be seen blooming gorgeously in several gardens and my travelling companions all begged for seeds.

The genus *Mimulus* belongs to the Scrophulariaceae, or Figwort Family, along with the more prosaic snapdragon, *Antirrhinum*, and foxglove, *Digitalis*. *Mimulus* is comprised of some 150 species of spring and summer annual and perennial herbs, or shrubs, native to South Africa, Asia, Australia, and the Americas, particularly western North America. *Mimulus cardinalis* is likely more tolerant of summer heat and an occasional dry spell than the more commonly grown mimulus pictured in seed catalogues, which are treated as annuals and require a relatively cool climate and rich, evenly moist soil.

MIMULUS CARDINALIS (above), IS SEEN IN LATE SUMMER WITH DWARF BLUE FESCUE IN A PORTLAND, OREGON, GARDEN. *PHLOMIS FRUTICOSA* (opposite), OR JERUSALEM SAGE, GROWN FOR ITS DENSELY WHITE-HAIRED LEAVES CROWNED BY WHORLS OF BRIGHT YELLOW FLOWERS, IS SEEN HERE AT CALLAWAY GARDENS IN GEORGIA.

MONARDA CITRIODORA

Lemon mint, *Monarda citriodora*, is native to the limestone regions of South Carolina and Florida, west to Missouri, Texas, and Mexico. It blooms the first year from seed, and the erect stems 18 to 24 inches tall are clothed in spring and summer with lemon-scented leaves toward the bottom and, toward the top, with showy lavender-pink flowers quite different from the usual garden cultivars of *M. didyma* (bee balm).

PHLOMIS FRUTICOSA

Last winter I saw numerous species of *Phlomis* glistening with frost at the Chelsea Physic Garden in London. By late May, when I came back for a second visit, the plants greeted me with a fresh crop of gray leaves and a great showing of yellow flowers in whorls. There are approximately a hundred different species of *Phlomis*, all closely related to the sage of herbalists, *Salvia officinalis*, and native from the Mediterranean region east to central Asia and China. In writer Ann Lovejoy's garden in Washington, Jerusalem sage makes a lovely combination in autumn with the finely divided leaves of Russian sage, *Perovskia atriplicifolia*, and the violet-purple berries of beautyberry, *Callicarpa*. Considering its obviously attractive gray leaves, and very yellow flowers, it is surprising not more gardeners grow Jerusalem sage. Perhaps a misunderstanding of its sub-shrub status is to blame, but the plant actually appreciates much the same care as ordinary sage, or almost any herbaceous perennial.

POLYGONUM BISTORTA 'SUPERBUM' HAS MOSTLY
BASAL LEAVES FROM WHICH ARISE DENSE SPIKES
OF PINK FLOWERS. SINCE THE DRIED RHIZOMES
HAVE BEEN USED MEDICINALLY, THIS PERENNIAL
IS SOMETIMES FOUND IN HERB GARDENS.

POLYGONUM BISTORTA 'SUPERBUM'

Polygonum bistorta 'Superbum', or showy bistort, is a cultivar of
a northern European and Asian herb, the dried rhizomes of
which have been used in herbal medicine. The species' common name, snakeweed, suggests a particular use and explains
why we often discover this flowering plant in herb gardens. A
specimen on display at the Brooklyn Botanic Garden has
helped popularize the showy bistort among the avid gardeners
in the region.

Since today we are more likely to admire 'Superbum' than
to dry its roots to treat snakebite, it is included here with
other prized perennials. In late spring the plant produces pink
flowers in dense spikes, to about 30 inches tall, and continues
to bloom sporadically until autumn. Give it well-drained,
humusy soil in full to half sun.

Polygonum is comprised of about 150 annuals and perennials,
widely distributed and including the graceful silver lace vine,
P. aubertii, as well as some weeds. The genus includes the edible Vietnamese-mint or false coriander, *P. odoratum*, discussed
in Chapter Three, and the fast-growing Japanese knotweed or
Mexican bamboo, *P. cuspidatum*, which is covered in Chapter
Six. There are also low-growing groundcovers such as *P. affine*,
with tufted pale green leaves and ten-inch spikes of rosy
flowers during late summer and autumn, and a cultivar, 'Dar-
jeeling Red', which in late summer bears erect spikes of rosy
pink blossoms that darken to a full-bodied red. All these,
along with such surprising relatives as coral vine, *Antigonon lep-
topus*, and rhubarb, *Rheum*, belong to the Buckwheat Family, as
does *Fagopyrum esculentum*, the source of buckwheat flour.

REHMANNIA ELATA

Rehmannia has been cherished by gardeners for at least half a century and is the subject of current breeding efforts at the University of British Columbia Botanical Garden in Vancouver. These tender Asiatic perennials have coarsely toothed, alternate leaves and large showy flowers in gracefully drooping clusters. In frost-free gardens where summer heat isn't too hellish the plants grow easily in part shade and moist soil, and will bloom over a long period. *Rehmannia elata* (or *R. angulata*) is a hardy perennial from China. Breeding work is being done to expand the range and appeal of this unusual flower. The plant grows one to three feet high, with sparsely leaved, angled stems branching from the base. Its dark green, deeply toothed leaves form large spreading rosettes. The tubular scarlet flowers, three inches across, have orange dots inside the lower lip. In the cultivar 'Tigrina' the flowers are more prominently spotted. 'Tricolor' has flowers that open bright purple, then turn violet-rose with a whitish throat. Gardeners in cold temperate regions may grow rehmannias in pots sunk into the garden in dappled sun in summer, and moved to a cool greenhouse or window garden in winter. To most gardeners rehmannia in bloom is a handsome plant. But taxonomists can't seem to make up their minds about it, classifying it first as a gesneriad, then as a scrophulariad. Rehmannia also bears a curious resemblance to a plant called hardy gloxinia, *Incarvillea delavayi*, that belongs to neither of the previously mentioned families but to the Bignonia Family. Besides a confusion of names, an important difference is that *Incarvillea* is hardy, to 0°F. or colder. Hardy gloxinia has pinnate, fern-like leaves, to 12 inches, with many leaflets. In early summer, the flower stalk rises about two feet above the foliage, and bears clusters of yellow or red blossoms with yellow tubes, about two inches long.

REHMANNIA ELATA HAS FLOWERS WHICH ARE REMINISCENT OF HARDY GLOXINIA. IT GROWS TO THREE FEET TALL IN A SINGLE SEASON, AND IN COLD CLIMATES MUST BE WINTERED OVER IN A FROST-FREE PLACE.

RHEUM

To the average person, the epitome of adventurous gardening may be to grow rhubarb as an ornamental. But to enlightened gardeners the idea is not so strange. The rhubarb pie plant is *Rheum rhaponticum*, which has large round basal leaves that are quite poisonous, and edible leafstalks 15 to 30 inches long, typically cheery, bright cherry red in color. As a hardy perennial producer of an edible crop the utilitarian rhubarb plant is often planted in a row at the edge of the kitchen garden. There it makes quite a nice hedge all summer, but its efforts to flower are usually literally nipped in the bud. On the other hand, *R. palmatum* 'Atrosanguineum' deserves a prominent place among other ornamentals in the flower garden or shrubbery border, to be cherished for its reddish and olive-green leaves that are divided like the fingers of a hand. The rather astonishing flower clusters appear in early summer at the end of the central stalk, which grows to five or six feet high. Whether grown for show or food, rhubarb does best with a half day or more of direct sun, in rich, moist soil that is generously top-dressed over winter with well-rotted manure. It is a mistake ever to plant any rhubarb where its roots will have to compete with large trees or encroaching weeds.

RHEUM PALMATUM 'ATROSANGUINEUM' IS A RHUBARB GROWN IN FLOWER GARDENS FOR THE ORNAMENTAL EFFECT OF ITS LEAVES, SEEN HERE IN THEIR IMPOSING GLORY IN THE COMPANY OF *EUONYMUS FORTUNEI* 'EMERALD 'N GOLD', A HIGHLY VARIEGATED WINTERCREEPER.

SALVIA GREGII

Autumn sage, *Salvia greggii*, has gained new respect for its role in Xeriscaping (drought-tolerant gardening) in areas where winter temperatures stay above 25°F. Autumn sage is lightly shrubby, growing to two or three feet high. Beginning in mid-summer and continuing through autumn, the species puts on a constant display of showy rose-red flowers; varieties are also available with pink, white, peach, cherry, and raspberry flowers. This ornamental sage is easily propagated from cuttings, and like its relative, the rosemary of herbalists, it can be enjoyed in cold climates as a container plant that is placed outdoors in full sun in warm weather and brought indoors to a cool, sunny, airy environment in winter. When autumn sage finishes flowering in late autumn, any dried up racemes or excessive growth can be cut back. At the beginning of the new season in spring, cut back the plant by half or more.

SALVIA LEUCANTHA

Mexican bush sage, *Salvia leucantha*, grows waist-high by the end of summer, when it covers itself with long spires of velvety lavender and white flowers carried above the silvery leaves. It is an ideal perennial for Xeriscapes in mild climates where winters as a rule do not bring temperatures much below freezing. *Salvia leucantha* may also be grown in containers; a nice specimen can be cultivated in a 12-inch clay pot and treated to an indoor/outdoor life as described for *S. greggii*. In the ground or in pots, this salvia looks especially beautiful in the company of pink or rosy flowers, in particular some of the new shrub roses that are often at their best in early autumn when leucantha is a haze of silvery lavender. Chrysanthemums, Japanese anemones, and asters also make good companions.

SALVIA GREGGII (above), FROM TEXAS AND MEXICO, IS CALLED AUTUMN SAGE FOR ITS HABIT OF BLOOMING GENEROUSLY IN LATE SUMMER AND AUTUMN. FIVE COLORS ARE AVAILABLE, AS WELL AS PURE WHITE. LIKE *SALVIA LEUCANTHA* (opposite), *S. GREGGII* IS FOR MILD CLIMATES OR GARDENERS WITH GREENHOUSES. SIMILARLY DROUGHT-TOLERANT *S. LEUCANTHA*, MEXICAN BUSH SAGE, IS GLORIOUS IN EARLY AUTUMN.

TRACHELIUM CAERULEUM

This relatively obscure member of the Bellflower Family is something of an amethyst-blue version of *Centranthus ruber* (of the Valerian Family). It grows to three feet tall and blooms from summer into autumn. Trachelium looks good with almost any other flower, including *Salvia leucantha*, and with gold, chartreuse, or silver foliage. The plant is perennial in the Deep South; elsewhere treat it as an annual. Grow it from seeds

started early each season, or dig and cut back selected plants before heavy frost in autumn, pot them up and keep them in a frost-free cold frame or sun-heated pit in winter. The photographs here were taken in late September in the sunny herbaceous border at the Virginia Robinson Gardens in Beverly Hills.

TRACHELIUM CAERULEUM (above) AND WITH *SALVIA LEUCANTHA*, (right), IN EARLY AUTUMN.

CHAPTER
TWO

INTRIGUING
ANNUALS

An annual by strict definition is a plant that completes its life cycle — from seed to bloom and back to seed — in a single season. In practice, the category includes hardy annuals, half-hardy annuals, tender perennials treated as annuals, and hardy perennials that grow from seed to bloom in one season. It also includes biennial plants that grow from seed one year for blooms the next, but which may bloom the first year from seed and which also have the habit of self-sowing, so that once established they regenerate with little more care than a hardy perennial. Many of the plants in this chapter are labor-intensive, requiring a certain amount of fussing over at the beginning of every growing season. Since this is true of annuals in general, the bedding plant industry provides us with seedlings already established in convenient packs. Because color at the pack stage sells plants, breeders have been asked to produce hybrids that are ever earlier blooming, preferably on plants short of stature. Serious gardeners have come to look upon these plants with approximately the same disdain as the gourmet cook regards convenience foods. Hardly any plant included in this chapter can be found in packs at a local nursery or garden center. The seeds of most are listed in one or more catalogues and planting guidelines are included in the text. Another notion

that doesn't necessarily flatter the annual is that it is temporary, a stop-gap measure to fill up the holes between perennial flowers or shrubs until they become established sufficiently to fill their allotted space in the border. But today's leading garden designers choose annuals for color, texture and habit, mixing and matching them with perennials, ornamental grasses and shrubbery, not once thinking of them as mere filler until something better comes along.

There is a fine line between annuals considered folk plants and those that suit the adventurous gardener. The old-fashioned four o'clock, Mirabilis jalapa, is a perfect example. It is not very widely grown, but seeds can be bought from catalogues and local racks. The delicate, textured flowers open fresh daily, around four o'clock in the afternoon, in white, shades of yellow, gold, orange, pink, and red, and in bicolors. Perhaps their greatest asset is the unique and pleasant perfume they give off, most pronounced on a warm summer's evening. Though usually grown as annuals, the plants do form tuberous roots deep in the ground, weighing more than forty pounds when grown as perennials in warm climates. The four o'clock definitely has a place in cottage gardens, and it is a trooper in the tough conditions of the inner city. Is it a plant for adventurous gardeners? Only the adventurous will know.

NOLANA NAPIFORMIS 'SKY BLUE' (previous two pages) IS A CULTIVAR
OF CHILEAN BELLFLOWER, A SOUTH AMERICAN PERENNIAL
GROWN AS AN ANNUAL IN COLD CLIMATES. VERBENA RIGIDA
'POLARIS' (RIGHT), A PERENNIAL TREATED AS AN ANNUAL, HAS
POWDER-BLUE FLOWERS ON 12-INCH PLANTS ALL SUMMER.
HERE IT GROWS WITH PINK PETUNIAS.

ALTHAEA ZEBRINA

Miniature hollyhock is known variously as *Althaea zebrina*, *Malva 'Zebrina'*, and *Malva sylvestris*. A European biennial by horticultural classification, it has naturalized in the United States and when cultivated behaves perfectly as an annual, blooming profusely from midsummer to frost from seeds started early indoors. This little hollyhock shares several traits associated

with other plants in this book, including questionable identity, garden performance at odds with its classification, and a habit of producing great quantities of seeds that gardeners generously share, thus devaluing the plant to those whose interest is purely commercial. Zebrina leaves are not rustproof but they are definitely resistant to the disease. The plants grow to three feet and require no staking or deadheading. They are drought tolerant, in the ground or in large pots.

AMARANTHUS CAUDATUS

Everyone knows *Amaranthus caudatus* as love-lies-bleeding, a name inspired by the long, slender, drooping flower spikes, reminiscent of the chenille plant, *Acalypha hispida*; but, as they belong to different botanical families, they are dissimilar when closely compared. Love-lies-bleeding came originally from the tropics and is cultivated in India as a food plant — for the young leaves and seeds — which is why this curious annual may be found growing in collections of herbs. In North American gardens, especially toward the South, it may become naturalized, in which case the young seedlings transplant easily. Being shallow-rooted, established plants must not be disturbed by cultivating too deeply around them. Rich, constantly moist soil may encourage a rank habit at the expense of flower quantity and color. Mild stress, from lean soil and slight drying at the surface between waterings, results in the most saturated coloring of flowers and the rosy stems. Plants grow four to five feet tall by the end of the summer. 'Green Thumb' is one-third to one-half this height and has clover green flower spikes. 'Pygmy Torch' is also dwarf, with unusually large blood-red flowers. (These two cultivars are variously listed in catalogues and references as belonging to either *A. caudatus* or *A. hypochondriacus*.)

A closely related plant which glows in the garden from midsummer on is *Amaranthus tricolor salicifolius*, also known as willow-leaved tampala or fountain plant. It takes its variety name, *salicifolius*, from the narrow, twisting leaves, which resemble those of willows (the botanical name for willow is *Salix*). Plain tampala is grown in the Orient as a green vegetable; the cultivar *A. t.* 'Splendens' and other varietal forms are the familiar annual Joseph's-coats. They range from two to six feet tall, and the upper third of the plants is painted in various combinations of rose, scarlet, and yellow.

ALTHEA ZEBRINA (opposite and above) IS A MINIATURE HOLLYHOCK
TREATED AS AN ANNUAL WHICH GROWS TO THREE FEET TALL. WITH AN
ABUNDANCE OF ONE-INCH PURPLE-STRIPED LAVENDER FLOWERS
FROM MIDSUMMER TO FROST FROM SPRING-SOWN SEEDS, IT NEEDS NO STAKING

LOVE-LIES-BLEEDING (above) IS *AMARANTHUS CAUDATUS*, AN ANNUAL CULTIVATED IN INDIA AS A FOOD PLANT FOR ITS YOUNG LEAVES AND SEEDS. 'PYGMY TORCH' (right), A CULTIVAR THAT GROWS HALF AS TALL, TO TWO FEET, HAS LARGER, MORE VIVIDLY COLORED FLOWERS.

THE GREEN FORM OF *AMARANTHUS TRICOLOR*
SALICIFOLIUS, (above) WILLOW-LEAVED TAMPALA
OR ANNUAL JOSEPH'S-COAT, IS GROWN AS A
VEGETABLE IN THE ORIENT. THE LEAVES BECOME
MORE BRILLIANT IF THE PLANTS ARE GROWN IN
LEAN, NOT OVERLY RICH SOIL.

CHENOPODIUM BOTRYS

This is the *Ambrosia mexicana* of horticulture, also known as Jerusalem oak (the leaves of self-sown seedlings in the spring suggest those of a tiny oak tree) and feather geranium. Alice Morse Earle, the revered early twentieth century American garden writer, recalled, "Ambrosia was my mother's favorite, hence it is mine. It was her favorite because she loved its pure, spicy fragrance. . . . This ever-present and ever-welcome scent (which pervades the entire garden if leaf or flower of the loved ambrosia be crushed) is curious and characteristic" — a true "ambrosiack odor" to use Ben Jonson's words.

Adelma Grenier Simmons introduced me to ambrosia at Caprilands Herb Farm, her mecca for herb lovers in Coventry, Connecticut. She describes the plant in her contemporary classic, *Herb Gardening in Five Seasons*, explaining that the plant's delicate, feathery leaves give it the appearance of "a lime-green plume" when it is mature. Sprigs of fresh ambrosia are used to flavor gin drinks, and longer branches make an aromatic filler for all manner of fresh flower bouquets, especially when combined with bolder forms such as zinnias or full-blown garden roses. Mrs. Simmons prefers ambrosia for dried wreaths and winter arrangements, advising gardeners to cut branches filled to the seed stage and place them to air-dry in vases without water. If the vases are placed out of the sun, the ambrosia will retain a beautiful green color as it dries. Mrs. Simmons also notes that the most difficult thing about ambrosia is that novice growers may mistake its seedlings for weeds.

If you decide to try your hand at growing ambrosia, be advised that working it into a garden with other plants will require subtle artistry since in full growth it has a tendency to resemble piles of green knots, as if turned helterskelter from a tatter's basket. But staking ambrosia is as unthinkable as not growing it, so give it plenty of room to sprawl.

AMBROSIA THE PLANT (NOT AMBROSIA THE FRUIT DESSERT) IS *CHENOPODIUM BOTRYS*, ALSO KNOWN AS JERUSALEM OAK AND FEATHER GERANIUM. SPRIGS OF ITS LEAVES CAN BE USED TO FLAVOR GIN DRINKS.

AMBROSIA, WHICH GROWS TO TWO FEET, IS
FRAGRANT AND DECORATIVE WITH OTHER
FLOWERS, HERE ZINNIA AND 'FERNLEAF' DILL. IT
ALSO DRIES TO A SUBTLE GREEN COLOR, MOST
WELCOME IN WINTER BOUQUETS.

CIRSIUM JAPONICUM

The thistle flower in profile is a classic design element that, for some gardeners, adds charisma to *Cirsium japonicum*, the Japanese thistle. Many other gardeners are put off by the mere mention of the word "thistle". It makes them think of unpleasant, even loathsome weeds. For gardeners who are kindly disposed to thistles, the chief drawback to Japanese thistle is that it blooms late. 'Early Beauty Hybrids', a recent development, does not require long daylength to set buds, but instead flowers early in the season from seeds started indoors six to eight weeks before planting-out time. While the species form of Japanese thistle grows to three feet or more, the Early Beauties top out at two feet and bloom freely over a long season. The individual quill-petaled flowers are white, pink, or rose, to two inches across. They are elegant in a sunny border and outstanding cut flowers. Also on the market are seeds of 'Early Pink Beauty' and 'Early Rose Beauty', both said to grow 30 inches tall from perennial rhizomes hardy to well below 0°F.

COSMOS 'SEASHELLS'

'Seashells' is a cosmos flower with a difference. Each petal is tubular, flaring at the tip into a trumpet. The colors — crimson, pink, dark rose with a crimson zone, and white — are typical of *Cosmos bipinnatus*, a Mexican species that blooms most gloriously as the days grow shorter toward frost. 'Seashells', to three feet tall and half as wide, is in full bloom much earlier, and is coveted for cutting. It is genetically stable so that seeds saved produce plants like the parents. Sow in a sunny site, in well-drained, moist soil; they are drought tolerant once they become established.

FIRECRACKER PLANT, *CUPHEA IGNEA*, GOES OFF IN
A BURST OF COLOR, HERE AT BUTCHART
GARDENS, BRITISH COLUMBIA, IN AUTUMN.

CUPHEA IGNEA

Firecracker plant seems the most apt common name for *Cuphea ignea* (or *C. platycentra*), also known as cigar flower and red-white-and-blue flower. Native to Mexico and Jamaica, it is an herbaceous or lightly shrubby tender perennial that can be treated as an annual except in frost-free gardens. This member of the Loosestrife Family is an example of a flower without any petals, only a scarlet, tubular calyx, with a dark blue ring at the end and a white tip. (*C. hyssopifolia*, the recently popular elfin-herb or false-heather, is a related plant whose flower has six equal petals.)

Seeds started indoors in a warm, sunny place or under lights six to eight weeks before frost danger is past bloom all summer. If given a modicum of care during the dog days, perhaps lightly cutting them back and providing the equivalent of an inch of rainfall a week in dry weather, the plants will flower more intensely at the beginning of September and into early autumn. Cuphea delights children of all ages, and at least one or two seedlings ought to be set in pots or planters.

Do not confuse cuphea with two tropical plants in the genus *Manettia*, called firecracker vine.

DYSSODIA TENUIFOLIA

The charming and cheery yellow Dahlberg daisy is a low-spreading to bushy annual, or a short-lived perennial in mild-climate gardens, that grows just eight inches tall. It goes all to bloom in four months from seed, which you may find for sale as *Thymophylla tenuiloba* (referring to the thyme-scented ferny leaves). Give the Dahlberg daisy well-drained, sandy soil in full sun. Myriad one-inch daisies look their best spilling onto a garden path or over the edge of a basket or window box.

EMILIA JAVANICA

Tassel-flower or paintbrush is sometimes listed in catalogues as *Cacalia coccinea*. Older references may use *Emilia sagittata* instead of the current *E. javanica*. The wild species is native to the tropics of both hemispheres and has naturalized in southern Florida. Selections offered by seed companies are freer blooming, have somewhat larger flowers in brighter hues — orange, scarlet, yellow, gold — and are sometimes available in separate colors. Emilia forms first a cluster of leaves that rises about six inches from the ground, then begins sending up erect flowering stems to two feet, topped by one-inch tassel-like flowers that are attractive in the garden as they wave in the breeze, and may be cut for fresh or dried bouquets.

Sow seeds indoors in March and transplant when the weather is warm, for early bloom beginning in June and continuing to frost. Or sow outdoors where the plants are to grow, as soon as the soil has warmed. Emilia adapts readily to sandy loam, full sun, and well-drained, rather dry locations, thriving even near the seashore. It self-sows freely and reappears each year. Under just the right set of conditions emilia has been known to become too much of a good thing, but unwanted seedlings can be easily pulled from moist soil and contributed to the compost pile.

THE NAMES TASSEL FLOWER AND FLORA'S-PAINTBRUSH SUIT *EMILIA JAVANICA*,

SEEN HERE IN EARLY SUMMER AT THE BROOKLYN BOTANIC GARDEN.

EUPHORBIA MARGINATA

Snow-on-the-mountain, *Euphorbia marginata* (referred to in some sources as *E. variegata*), grows wild from Minnesota to Colorado and Texas. The photograph shows one in August, in a buffalo grass pasture in the Oklahoma Panhandle. This annual snow-on-the-mountain. It is the white-margined leaves that are eye-catching, not the unobtrusive flowers.

A similar species, annual poinsettia, named for upper leaves and bracts that are red or red-based, may be *E. cyathophora* or

needs damp soil in spring for the seeds to sprout, and sufficient ground moisture to draw the roots downward. Thereafter snow-on-the-mountain is a drought-buster. *Euphorbia marginata* is listed as two feet tall, but in my travels, I have seen it twice this high and as wide as both arms can reach. Gardeners fond of variegated leaves will have no trouble finding a place for

E. heterophylla; other names are fire-on-the-mountain, Mexican fire plant, and mole plant. Be forewarned: Euphorbias may release into the soil in their vicinity alkaloids not friendly to other plants. For this reason they are often grown alone as accents or as annual hedging. Also, the milky latex from euphorbias can cause skin irritation.

GILIA CAPITATA

Queen Anne's thimble, *Gilia capitata*, is a wildflower from the western United States that grows gracefully to 30 inches and produces sky blue, one-inch flowerheads like rounded powder-puffs, on long stems. Gilia looks beautiful and enhances the appearance of almost any plant or color in its vicinity; flower arrangers love working with its long stems. While the spring weather is still cool enough to plant radishes and leaf lettuce, sow gilia seeds in a sunny site where they are to grow. I found the plant blooming in late August in Vermont after more tender plants had succumbed to frost. Curiously, a wholesale seed catalogue issued in 1992 describes *G. capitata* as "new." "To whom?" I wonder, for the species was described in detail in *Hortus Third*, which was published in 1976.

EUPHORBIA MARGINATA (opposite), IS A NORTH AMERICAN NATIVE. *GILIA CAPITATA* (above) WITH FLANDER'S FIELD POPPY (*PAPAVER RHOEAS*) BLOOMS ALL SUMMER. THE PASTEL ANNUAL SUNFLOWER (below) IS *HELIANTHUS ANNUUS* 'AUTUMN GIANT'.

HELIANTHUS ANNUUS

Everybody smiles at the sunflower. Lately it has become so synonymous with country life that small bouquets of cut blossoms command big prices in the city. The seed industry has responded by breeding new cultivars that can be divided into three basic types. The one-flower group, *H. annuus*, two to 10 feet tall, produces one large, golden yellow flower, single or double, to 10 inches across, and a few small ones per plant. The branching group, *H. debilis* (cucumberleaf sunflower), produces many more flowers, but smaller, to four inches across, in yellow, gold, bronze, brown, and mahogany, on plants to five feet high. The branching hybrids combine both species to produce plants to seven feet tall and many long-stemmed flowers to eight inches across, in all the colors previously mentioned and in pastel blends atypical of the sunflower.

KOCHIA SCOPARIA

Summer cypress, *Kochia scoparia* 'Childsii', is a dense green
plant that grows from seed to 30 inches tall by midsummer. At
first glance this surprising annual appears to be a well-formed
evergreen shrub. Summer cypress has long been recommended
as a temporary hedge, with seedlings planted 12 inches apart
for this purpose. Kochia is described as "a bad weed if allowed
to go to seed" in a 1986 catalogue from a company no longer
in business. Indeed, kochias belong to the Goosefoot Family,
along with ambrosia, lamb's-quarters, garden orach — and some
of the world's more congenial weeds.

Another form of the plant, called *K. s. trichophylla*, turns purplish red in autumn, and is popularly known as burning bush,
firebush, or red summer cypress. A current catalogue notes
that the foliage of *K. s.* 'Childsii' also turns scarlet in autumn.
The white variegated cultivar shown in the photograph, 'Acapulco Silver', is one of the relatively small number of plants
having variegated leaves that comes true from seeds. If an appreciation of ordinary kochia can be considered adventurous,
then 'Acapulco Silver' is practically beyond the pale.

LAVATERA 'TANAGRA'

Satin rose mallow, *Lavatera trimestris*, is a half-hardy annual that can be sown where it is to bloom as soon as the ground can be worked in the spring. As the weather warms and days grow longer, lavatera seedlings shift into high gear, soon becoming shrubby plants covered with silken, flaring cup flowers to four inches across. 'Tanagra' bears glowing carmine-rose flowers on plants three feet tall. There are also 'Loveliness' (dark pink, to four feet), 'Mont Blanc' (white, to two feet) and 'Silver Cup' (salmon pink with darker veins, to two feet).

Lavatera plants need constant moisture early on until they are established, then they can be quite drought tolerant if given an organic mulch two to four inches deep. Apart from their attractive form and habit, the flowers are lovely over a very long season, appearing as fresh on a hot summer evening as on a misty autumn morning.

MATTHIOLA BICORNIS

Everyone is familiar with the giant, mammoth or column stock, the ones professionals coax into bloom in cool climates and which are irresistible as cut flowers. Less known is evening-scented stock, *Matthiola bicornis*, which grows to 20 inches tall and bears small, mauve, mustard-type flowers that might go unnoticed were it not for the scent they give off from late afternoon into the night. Evening-scented stock is the perfect snippet of bloom to slip into a little bouquet next to a bed, or in the bath. Plant seeds as described for lavatera (above), in a spot that receives a half-day or more of sun. This wildling stock may not exactly love a muggy day but no matter, by dinner time it will be scenting the air as if contented.

NICOTIANA RUSTICA

NICOTIANA RUSTICA WAS THE FIRST TOBACCO
INTRODUCED TO THE OLD WORLD. IT GROWS TO
THREE FEET TALL AND IS GROWN TODAY FOR
PANICLES OF GREENISH YELLOW FLOWERS.
WHITE NIGELLA (opposite) COMES ALSO IN PALE
BLUE AND IN THE LARGER, DOUBLE BLUE 'MISS
JEKYLL,' THE LATTER A FAVORITE OF GERTRUDE
JEKYLL. THE SCALLOPED, QUILTED LEAVES
ARE THE HERB BETONY.

This species was the first tobacco brought to the Old World by Jean Nicot, French ambassador to Portugal, who introduced it to France and bequeathed his name to the genus, *Nicotiana*. Originally from the Andes, ranging from what is now Ecuador to Bolivia, *N. rustica* grows to over three feet tall and produces panicles of greenish yellow tubular flowers with five short lobes. *Hortus Third* says this is the original tobacco, smaller and hardier than *N. tabacum* and grown in pre-Columbian times by Indians of Mexico and eastern North America, later by the Virginia colonists. At one time it was grown in Europe and Asia for the production of nicotine insecticide and for fumigation. The leaves vary from oval heart-shaped to elliptic, and from four to eight inches long. The *N. rustica* pictured was flowering in midsummer in a border at Clark Botanical Garden in Albertson, New York. The leaves and plants make a bold statement from some distance, and up close, the pale green blossoms are lovely. Gardeners interested in the unusual grow it as a curiosity and as a foil for colorful flowers and finely textured leaves. Candlestick flowering tobacco, *N. sylvestris*, grows rapidly in warm summer weather and almost overnight bursts into spectacular bloom, each stalk rising to as much as six feet and crowned with hundreds of long white tubular flowers that give off an intoxicating perfume. Except in the coldest climates these nicotianas have the fortunate habit of self-sowing just the right amount; they are never weedy. Except for a little thinning in early summer, maybe transplanting some seedlings to other parts of the garden, this plant reappears year after year with almost no bother. Because of its commanding height, *N. sylvestris* is best at the back of a border or near the wall of a cottage garden. It can also be scattered to romantic effect in a nearly wild area.

NIGELLA DAMASCENA

Love-in-a-mist and fennel flower are folk names for *Nigella damascena*, a half-hardy annual from the Mediterranean region and western Asia. Feathery, fennel-like leaves, blue or white spidery flowers to two inches across, and a strong constitution make this a favorite for all kinds of gardens — herb, cottage, kitchen cutting, and on the wild side. The plants grow to two feet and the flowers stand up well. The seedpods of flowers left standing can be cut for dried arrangements.

Sow seeds in early spring where the plants are to grow; making several successive sowings will extend the flowering season. Nigella self-sows nicely in well-drained garden soil and a sunny site; thin seedlings to six inches apart. 'Miss Jekyll' is the cultivar most offered in catalogues, with semi-double to fully double flowers in azure blue, named for its patron saint, Gertrude Jekyll, the English artist-gardenmaker-author of a century past. Without her name the nigella would be no less lovely, but far less known. How could anyone turn away 'Miss Jekyll' and once invited in, who could neglect her needs for water and a bit of loving care? 'Mulberry Rose' has been recently introduced from the Netherlands. Its clear dark rose flowers are larger, as are the seedpods, which in turn are striped with purple-rose.

PAPAVER

The annual species *Papaver somniferum* cannot be grown legally in the United States because it is the opium poppy. But hybridized strains having large, many-petaled flowers to more than three inches across are showy — and legal. There are two types, *P. s.* 'Paeonia Flowered Hybrids', which grows to four feet tall and yields smooth-edged, double flowers like peonies in similar colors (white to rose and lavender), and *P. s.* 'Florepleno', whose frilled petals are responsible for the name carnation poppy.

These poppies are hardy annuals raised from seeds sown outdoors in late summer or early autumn in warmer regions, in early spring elsewhere. They require full sun and light, sandy, well-drained loam. Sow the seeds where the plants are to bloom. It is vital to thin any crowded plants, or the poppies will be stunted. The numbers of self-sown seedlings can be reduced and the current flowering season extended by deadheading spent blooms. Because of the illegality of the species *Papaver somniferum*, many seed companies will have nothing to do with this poppy in any form. A gardening friend is the usual source for this plant.

PHACELIA CAMPANULARIA

California bluebell is a descriptive name for *Phacelia campanularia*, a heat- and drought-tolerant annual growing to 20 inches tall that is native to Colorado and the Mojave deserts of southern California. The catalogue for J.L. Hudson, Seedsman, Redwood City, California, calls this species desert bluebells, and the specific name, *campularia*, refers to the bell-shaped flowers. Hudson notes that the stems and leaf edges are often red, and are fragrant when bruised.

The showiest specimens I have seen were at a seed company in the Lompoc Valley, in the central part of California. This area typically has cool nights and pleasantly warm, sunny days, often without rain for most if not all of the summer. *Phacelia* has been in and out of catalogues and listings of "new" plants for as long as seedsmen have gone looking for new things to entice and please their customers. This beautiful wildflower apparently needs no pampering; give up regular watering and fertilizing if phacelia is to succeed. Sow the seeds in earliest spring where they are to mature, in a sunny place. Avoid any site involving sticky clay or otherwise poorly drained soil, as well as pockets of stale air or any condition inviting rot of root or limb. A large, shallow pot set on a ledge is ideal.

The hardy *P. tenacetifolia* grows to three feet, and has fern-shaped leaves and lavender-blue flowers that make excellent bee forage. Possibly the showiest is *P. viscida*, a hardy species from coastal California with one-inch flowers of gentian blue.

PAPAVER SOMNIFERUM (opposite) IS A SINGLE POPPY. IN *P. S.* 'PAEONIA FLOWERED HYBRIDS' OR PEONY POPPY, THE DOUBLE FLOWERS ARE VERY LARGE. MIGNONETTE (above), *RESEDA ODORATA*, SMELLS "CLEAN."

RESEDA ODORATA

Mignonette of perfumery is produced by distilling the essential oil from *Reseda odorata*, a North African native. The good news about mignonette is that it will do well with some shade; the bad news is that it needs cool nights (48°F. is the ideal greenhouse thermostat setting). Mignonette is often cultivated in pots for blooms indoors or out, depending on the season, the climate, and the gardener. 'Grandiflora' has cream flowers and grows to 24 inches. 'Grandiflora Machet' is reddish and half as tall. In either case, the goal is not so much a gorgeous

plant but a unique scent: country-fresh and clean. Reseda is a hardy annual that tolerates frost to a point. The seeds require light in order to sprout. Sow them on the soil surface, but take care to keep them uniformly moist throughout germination. Sow reseda directly in the garden or in pots, to avoid transplanting and disturbing its roots.

SALPIGLOSSIS SINUATA IS A HALF-HARDY ANNUAL

FROM CHILE WITH SHOWY FLOWERS IN A DAZZLING

VARIETY OF VENATIONS AND MARKINGS.

SALPIGLOSSIS SINUATA

Painted tongue is the common name for *Salpiglossis sinuata*, a Chilean annual belonging to the Nightshade Family. I have seen these magnificent blossoms in all their glory twice: in California's Lompoc Valley fields in midsummer, and during the third week of May at the Chelsea Flower Show in London. Salpiglossis can also be grown for winter display in a cool greenhouse from seeds planted in late summer. The trumpet blossoms, two to three inches long and as wide, range from apricot, buff, yellow, bronze, pale and dark browns to garnet reds, pale and dark blues, and royal purples. All are velvety and most are netted with gold veins.

TAGETES 'CINNABAR' IS ONE OF THE REDDEST MARIGOLDS YET, AN UNEXPECTED COLOR FOR A GENUS SYNONYMOUS WITH YELLOW, ORANGE, AND MAHOGANY. A MORE PUBLICIZED COLOR BREAKTHROUGH FOR *TAGETES* IS APPARENT IN THE LARGE-FLOWERED HYBRID WHITE MARIGOLDS, WHICH ARE ESPECIALLY LOVELY ON A MOONLIT EVENING.

Why is this flower so little known? One reason has to be the poor plant's unfortunate names: An invitation to see one's *Salpiglossis* is only slightly more appealing than to proffer one's painted tongue. The more serious matter has to do with temperature requirements, which are cool at night, around 48°F., and warm by day, up to 70° or so. When or where these needs can be met there is hardly any annual as splendid as the salpiglossis, for beds, borders, cutting, and containers. The plants, from one to three feet tall depending on the strain, need a half day of sun or more, rich soil that is deeply prepared, plenty of water, ideally applied at the roots, and staking.

TAGETES 'CINNABAR'

Is it possible for a marigold to be of esoteric interest? Yes, if it is a red form of the dwarf or French marigold, *Tagetes patula*, a most unusual color for this most familiar of plants. Yes again if it is pericon, *T. lucida*, a substitute for French tarragon (see Chapter Three). One of the reddest marigolds is 'Cinnabar', growing to 18 inches — tall enough for cutting — and single so

that the yellow center shines from the rich red petals. Another cultivar, 'Red Cherry', with smaller double flowers, grows a foot tall and blooms extra early. Red and scarlet flowers are available in the series Sophia, Safari, and Disco. Also of interest are the Signet marigolds, *T. tenuifolia* 'Pumila', which bear a profusion of dainty single flowers above lemon-scented, lacy foliage. Signet marigolds start blooming early and continue until frost, becoming mounds a foot tall and as wide.

VERBENA BONARIENSIS

The garden verbenas (*Verbena* $\times$ *hybrida*, sometimes *V. hortensis*) are of little interest to adventurous gardeners. There are, however, numerous verbena species, particularly those classed as vervains, that are in vogue among the most advanced and sophisticated of herbaceous border and cottage garden makers. Foremost is *V. bonariensis*, a South American perennial that is often grown as an annual. It reaches to four or five feet, with square stems that are much branched and long, narrow, toothed leaves and lavender or blue-purple flowers. This may sound like a lot of plant but in real life most of the leaves stay within a foot or so of the ground and the rest of the plant has long, slender stems and small clusters of flowers that hover in the air like moths or butterflies. These verbenas should be laced through other plantings, herbaceous or shrubby, of sturdier, stiffer habit. The upward-rising verbenas then provide a romantic scrimming that makes an impressionistic haze of otherwise harsh or too-vivid colors. Rose vervain, *V. canadensis*, is a perennial from the American Southwest and Mexico which grows to 18 inches, with a creeping rootstock and pink or purple blooms; it is especially nice for softening pathway edges. Blue vervain, *V. hastata*, common in the fields of North America, attains a height of three or four feet, and bears slender, straight, erect spikes of blue, white, pink, or lavender flowers. *Verbena rigida* grows upright to two feet and is a perennial that blooms generously the first year from seeds, with purple blossoms in spikes three inches long. In the cultivar 'Polaris' 12-inch plants are smothered for months on end in silvery-blue flowers. All of these vervains attract honeybees and butterflies. When established in a sunny to half-sunny site in well-drained soil they are drought-tolerant and root hardy to o°F. or colder.

ZINNIA ANGUSTIFOLIA

ZINNIA ANGUSTIFOLIA IS THE NARROW-LEAVED MEXICAN ZINNIA. 'STAR WHITE', FROM BURPEE, IS A WELCOME OPTION. THESE ZINNIAS BLOOM HEAVILY THROUGH MUGGY OR DRY WEATHER UNTIL FROST.

Some of the foremost gardeners admit to a lifelong love of the zinnia, because it is the first flower they grew as kindergarteners. At that age, when bigger and brighter often seem better, the California Giants were the ticket to a show with all the excitement of Jack and his beanstalk. Now worldly sophisticates, these same gardeners have learned that smaller zinnias can be even more fun, and so they search catalogues and lists of rare seeds for species such as *Zinnia angustifolia*. This Mexican native grows to 15 inches tall and spreads gracefully, spilling here and there, in an "at ease" posture that has been lost from the rigidly upright hybrids. Its single flowers, about an inch and a half across, are clear orange with a central yellow stripe that highlights their simple beauty. Another Mexican zinnia is *Z. haageana*, orange in the wild but bicolored red-and-yellow in cultivars 'Old Mexico' and 'Sombrero'. *Zinnia angustifolia* 'Star White', from Burpee, produces clouds of starry white flowers, to two inches across, from early summer to frost. An important reason to appreciate these little zinnias, and to invite them into the garden, is that the foliage is resistant to powdery mildew and alternaria (traditional zinnia problems), and the plants are rarely bothered by predatory insects, excessive heat, humidity, or protracted drought.

Zinnias need full sun, plenty of heat and moderately rich, friable soil. Sow seed outdoors when the ground is warm, about the same time when setting out tomatoes. For early flowers, sow indoors four weeks before planting-out weather.

In case there are any doubts about such an old shoe as the zinnia being of interest, remember that Vita Sackville-West, in quest of Peppermint Stick zinnias, wrote so many letters to her American pen pal Andrew Reiber that the correspondence became a book, *Dearest Andrew.* Presumably any flower coveted for the gardens at Sissinghurst is a flower worth growing.

CHAPTER
THREE

HERBS
AND
VEGETABLES

One of the major changes to occur in gardening in recent times is that many gardeners no longer relegate vegetables and other edibles to a separate growing area. Instead, they are now treated as garden-worthy subjects in any setting that suits their cultural needs. In history, useful edibles (vegetables and fruits) and medicinals (herbs) were the first plants to be cultivated; aesthetic qualities such as flowering and fragrance were considered incidental. In time, plants came to be divided into two groups: ornamentals, a sort of leisure class considered by many gardeners to be an expendable luxury, and edibles, a necessary working class that were not to be mingled with the ornamentals. Gardeners tended to have either edible or ornamental gardens. To some gardeners, any plant as serviceable as a vegetable deserved center-stage treatment. Others took the opposite view, that edibles were best grown in an out-of-the-way plot where they would fulfill their humble purpose but would not be seen or otherwise encountered socially. The beautiful food gardens promoted by such leading garden communicators as America's Rosalind Creasy and England's Rosemary Verey have made the enforced separation of edibles and ornamentals obsolete. Such intrepid gardeners have revealed a whole new way of seeing and using vegetables and herbs — as ornamentals in their own right. Creasy had the courage to plow up her front lawn in a proper San Francisco suburb and turn it into the food garden of her dreams, a garden that was as beautiful as it was productive. At first the neighbors looked askance, but they have come to admire and emulate her methods. Verey took a more historically inspired approach. She admired the superb artistry represented in the fabled kitchen gardens at Chateau Villandry in France, and found a way to translate it into a modest-sized space that suits and appeals to vast numbers of ordinary gardeners. The ways of Creasy and Verey can work their transformation on an ordinary container in a sawed-off whiskey barrel just as well as in a commodious space in the ground. The Japanese practice of koten engei (described in the Introduction) perhaps finds an edible gardener's counterpart in England's official Pot Leek Society, a group of gardeners who specialize in growing leeks in pots and bringing them to cultural perfection for entry in competitive exhibitions. If we follow the dictum, "love it, don't label it," then a potted leek is as valid — and beautiful — as an award-winning orchid or African violet. This chapter profiles a selection of unusual edibles possessed of distinctly ornamental properties. Some plants not included here are those whose flowers are edible: borage, calendula, chicory, gladiolus, hollyhock, honeysuckle, Johnny-jump-up, marigold, nasturtium, rose, runner bean, and squash.

MANY BASILS CARRY A GENE FOR PURPLE FOLIAGE (preceding pages) RECENT INTRODUCTION 'PURPLE RUFFLES' (far left in photo) RESEMBLES PERILLA. YELLOW-FLOWERED 'RED VELVET' OKRA (opposite) TURNS GREEN IF COOKED, BUT RETAINS ITS COLOR IF PICKLED.

ABELMOSCHUS ESCULENTUS

Okra, or gumbo, *Abelmoschus esculentus*, is an Asian tropical plant, with edible green, red, or white seedpods. Young pods can be eaten raw or used for tempura; larger ones can be sliced, dusted with corn meal, and fried in olive oil. When dried and roasted the seeds can be ground for a caffeine-free

ALLIUM CEPA

Egyptian onion, *Allium cepa viviparum*, belongs to the proliferum group of onions that proliferate or multiply by means of bulbils that develop in the flower cluster at the top of the plant. Gardeners can treat these bulbils as onion sets. Sometimes the tall stems may bend over and the bulbils root in the soil, a habit that inspired the old nickname of "walking onion." After the bulblets have formed, if the parents are cut back,

coffee substitute. Okra plants give a bold tropical appearance to the garden with the bonus of yellow flowers resembling mallow and hibiscus. In hot weather the plants grow from seed to mature height in a matter of weeks. The cultiver 'Red Velvet' grows to six feet, with dark red pods that turn green when cooked, and reddish ribbing in the leaves. 'Blondy' is a dwarf that grows up to three feet tall with creamy lime-colored pods.

they will grow again. Egyptian onion is a perennial that grows to three feet tall, and can be an interesting addition to a mixed border with other perennials. Plant in full sun, 12 inches apart in trenches six inches deep. As the shoots appear, gradually fill in the soil to produce a long, blanched stalk. Clip the young spears in spring for salads. The bulbils are small but intensely flavored and may be used like cloves of garlic.

ENGLISH LAVENDER, WHITE DAISY-LIKE CHAMOMILE (above), AND EGYPTIAN ONION (opposite) MAKE AN EFFECTIVE TRIO IN AN HERB GARDEN.

ALOYSIA TRIPHYLLA

Lemon verbena, *Aloysia triphylla* or *Lippia citriodora*, from Central and South America, is a member of the Verbena Family, cold hardy to about 10°F. It can grow to six feet or more as an indoor/outdoor container plant. Lemon verbena produces its leaves in whorls of three or four. They tend to be a pale yellowish green indoors but outdoors in fresh air and full sun, with ample nutrients and moisture, they grow dark green and take on a quilted texture. When brushed against they give off a lemony but haunting scent that is not quite like the fragrance of any other plant. The plant itself, by comparison to many ornamentals, is unremarkable; the blossoms are tiny, grayish white, and hardly noticeable. Lemon verbena's unique scent is the source of its charm. Harvest the leaves to dry for potpourri and to steep for tea. Rosalind Creasy, in *Cooking from the Garden*, suggests appropriating lemon verbena's strong lemon flavor for "a variety of dishes — fruit salads and drinks, jellies, chicken, and fish." The plant is wonderfully scented even as a rooted cutting. The finest specimen I have seen is a tree-form standard six feet tall that lives in an 18-inch terra cotta pot, spending summers along a path in the kitchen garden of C. Z. Guest. As one passes it, the branches invite touching. Before the first killing frost in autumn, lemon verbena should be moved into a sun-heated pit greenhouse or other protected location and kept cool until spring.

BETONICA OFFICINALIS

This member of the Mint Family is found in herb gardens, now usually under the botanical name of *Stachys officinalis*. Officinalis indicates a plant once used for medicinal purposes, and the folk names betony, hedge nettle, and woundwort also hint at this plant's herbal uses. At the Brooklyn Botanic Garden, where I have watched betony grow through the seasons, the basal rosettes of scalloped leaves attract the eye first. Later, in mid- to late summer, the dense spikes of red-purple flowers on slender stems to three feet tall could easily be mistaken for those of showy bistort. There is also a white-flowered cultivar, 'Alba'. Betony is the sort of plant that gets into the gardener's subconscious. It brings a welcome note of floral color to the summer herb garden. Betony's charmingly understated appearance also suggests its appropriateness for a sunny to half-sunny cottage or dooryard garden.

LEMON VERBENA TREE (opposite) GROWS IN THE LONG ISLAND KITCHEN GARDEN OF

C. Z. GUEST. BETONY (above) HAS SPIKES OF RED-PURPLE FLOWERS.

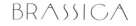

BRASSICA

Brassica is the genus name of an important and varied group of food plants from the Mustard or Crucifer Family. They are known also as borecoles. Ornamental forms of cabbage, with rounded, wavy-edged leaves, and kale, with frilled to frizzy-edged leaves (both *B. oleracea*, Acephala Group), have recently

become popular bedding and container plants for autumn and winter gardens. They are variegated in white to cream to blue-green and rosy purple, and give the effect of very large and double fantasy flowers. The latest discovery about them is that if the plants are left in place after winter, they will send up in spring or early summer racemes of decorative yellow flowers to two or three feet tall. Kohlrabi or stem-turnip, *B. oleracea*,

PURPLE KOHLRABI (above) IS ORNAMENTAL, EDIBLE, AND UNUSUAL. JAPANESE RED MUSTARD LEAVES (right) ARE BEST USED RAW IN SALADS AND SANDWICHES.

Gongylodes Group, has bluish green leaves to 18 inches that grow from an edible turnip-like tuber (actually a swollen stem) that forms above ground. In some cultivars, such as 'Early Purple Vienna', the tuber and leaf stalks are a glowing red-violet. The "bulbs" are best for eating when not more than two inches across, about two months after planting. Try them raw with a dip or cook them like turnips. The curious conformation of the plants is most apparent when they are planted in

raised beds. If the plants are not harvested for eating, they will produce racemes of pale yellow or cream-colored flowers.

The most recently discovered brassicas for adding color and attractive form to kitchen, container, and cottage gardens are the Japanese red mustards, *B. juncea*, such as 'Giant Red' and 'Osaka'. Rosalind Creasy rates them "showstoppers" and notes that the yellow flowers are also edible.

CAPSICUM ANNUUM

The red pepper is known in temperate climates as an annual but in warm regions such as its native tropical America the plants are woody perennials, some attaining eight feet in height (two is about the maximum for cultivated plants). Whether hot or sweet, garden peppers are all classified as *Capsicum annuum*, which botanists have sorted into five groups: cherry, cone, cluster, bell (including sweet, green, and pimento), and longum (capsicum, cayenne, chili, long, and red). There is in addition the bird pepper, *C. frutescens*, which is grown in the Gulf states for the production of hot sauce; hence it is also called "Tabasco pepper." *Hortus Third* mentions that certain cultivars of cherry, cone, and cluster peppers are grown as ornamentals, such as the popular Christmas pepper, which is sold at any time from late summer to early spring as a seasonal pot plant. And there is a multitude of other peppers to be grown from heirloom or hybrid seeds, purchased, collected, or bartered with other gardeners.

One cultivar of cone pepper has leaves highly variegated with white, purple, and pink. A cluster pepper ripening a generous crop of shiny, uniformly purple fruits from midsummer on can be an illustrious bedmate for any number of cottage garden dwellers. Cherry cultivar 'Holiday Cheer', with hot but edible fruit, looks like the related but poisonous ornamental, Jerusalem cherry, *Solanum pseudocapsicum*. Any believer in the concept of the food garden as beautiful will have no compunction about placing almost any pepper in the midst of more conventional ornamentals. The bell peppers, once taken for granted to be green until they matured to red, may also be had in lemon yellow, orange, purple, or chocolate brown. Gardeners who grow several different kinds of peppers and sow saved seeds find interesting variation in plant habit, from cascading to stiffly upright.

THE PURPLE PODS (opposite) AND THE FINGERY

FLAME-COLORED FRUITS (above) REPRESENT A

CLASS OF EDIBLE HOT PEPPERS THAT ARE

MARKETED AS ORNAMENTALS, OFTEN IN POTS.

CENTRANTHUS RUBER

Centranthus ruber, also known as Jupiter's-beard, keys of heaven, scarlet lightning, and red valerian, is sometimes included in the genus *Valeriana* (both are members of the Valerian Family). By any name it is a folk plant with a long history, a hardy perennial throughout much of the continental United States that blooms all summer.

The plant has a tidy, upright, and self-supporting habit, and grows to two or three feet high. Around the top are a multi-

tude of dome-shaped, fragrant flower clusters, which are usually rosy pink, but may also be found in a range of warm colors — crimson, scarlet, red, and pale pink — as well as lavender and white.

A Mediterranean native, red valerian was originally brought into cultivation for its generosity in perfuming the air, and it began to show up in proper herb gardens. Centranthus has become naturalized in parts of California even as cultivated strains are being named and sold by the finest nurseries.

Plantsman John Elsley notes that centranthus can be sheared back after the first wave of bloom, in order to promote intermittent flowering until the end of the growing season. This ability to repeat bloom made the plant eligible for a place in the United States National Arboretum's New American Garden in Washington, D.C.

The flowers are excellent for cutting and are seen increasingly in city flower stalls. In many regions centranthus fits also

ROSY *CENTRANTHUS RUBER*, OR RED VALERIAN, AND THE BLUE FLOWERS OF CATMINT (*NEPETA MUSSINII*) (left), SEEN HERE AT THE NEW YORK BOTANICAL GARDEN, ARE BECOMING STAPLES IN PERENNIAL FLOWER BORDERS. RADICCHIO (opposite) IS RED CHICORY, AS BEAUTIFUL IN THE FLOWER OR VEGETABLE GARDEN AS ON THE PLATE. BRAISED, ROASTED, GRILLED, OR RAW IN A SALAD.

into the concept of the Xeriscape — a garden that will require little if any irrigation in normal periods of dry weather. But almost everywhere centranthus can play a role in the most romantic cottage and beautiful food gardens.

Centranthus can be grown from seeds or, alternatively, from divisions taken from mature plants during spring. Be sure to site red valerian where it will get a half day or more of direct sun, in well-drained, compost-enriched soil that is loosened to the depth of a spade.

CICHORIUM INTYBUS

Travellers admiring the sky-blue flowers of wild chicory growing beside the road could hardly suspect that from the same genus and species, *Cichorium intybus*, also comes the red-leaved chicories that became something of a status symbol in chic salad bowls in the 1980s. They are cool-season crops started from seeds in spring or summer, and ready for harvest in autumn. The plants are allowed to grow all summer (when their leaves are mostly green), then in early autumn the leaves are cut off. The roots produce a second, smaller head with the rich burgundy leaves that are seen at the produce market. Traditionally, the heads are covered to produce the spectacular magenta coloring and white veining. The classic 'Treviso Red' dates back four or five centuries. Recently developed cultivars 'Giulio', 'Medusa', 'Alto', and 'Augusto' head up fairly well without cutting back as the autumn season advances.

CLAYTONIA PERFOLIATA

The interesting leaves of miner's lettuce, *Claytonia perfoliata* or *Montia perfoliata*, provide a classic example of a condition known as perfoliation, in which the base of each stalkless leaf completely surrounds the stem, making it appear to pass through the blade. At the juncture of leaf and stem on the upper surface, the plant bears racemes of very small, white flowers. Winter purslane and Cuban spinach are other names given to this salad plant and potherb. It grows wild from British Columbia to Mexico, and is easily raised from seeds sown in spring or summer directly where they are to grow. English gardener Rosemary Verey likes to contrast the glowing, fresh bright green of miner's lettuce against the blue-green or grayish foliage of leeks.

DRACOCEPHALUM MOLDAVICA

Dragonhead is the popular name for this genus of some 45 species belonging to the Mint Family. *Dracocephalum moldavica* is an annual, growing 24 to 36 inches tall, with fragrant foliage and, beginning in midsummer, lavender-purple or white flowers in elongated clusters at the tips of the stems. Bees find dragonhead plants in full bloom irresistible. On a warm day the air will be filled with their buzzing and the scent of the

plants themselves. Most dragonheads in general need humus-rich, moist soil and some shade. But *D. moldavica*, being originally from cold regions of the Northern Hemisphere, sprouts early in cool conditions, then really gets up and grows in hot weather. Unlike most of its relatives, this species is a good candidate for either Xeriscaping or container culture. Shear back the plants after the first flush of bloom to encourage more flowering later on. In adequate sunlight and air circulation *D. moldavica* forms symmetrical clumps of upright plants that need no staking. The blossoms are also self-cleaning.

FOENICULUM VULGARE

The feathery, finely cut leaves of ordinary green fennel, which rise to five feet, are distinctive enough to be grown with ornamentals by any gardener who doesn't know the rule about keeping edible plants off to themselves. The bronze-leaved form is even more outstanding, and is appearing in more and more flower gardens. When Rosemary Verey plants it with orange tulips in her gardens at Barnsley House and thousands of gardening devotees from around the world come to see what

she has put together, you can be sure bronze fennel's stock goes up. Fennel, whether green or bronze, grows easily from seeds sown in cold regions in summer for autumn harvest, elsewhere in autumn for spring growth. *Foeniculum vulgare* does best in a soil with a pH near neutral (7.0), well-spaded at planting and adequately supplied with water; it prefers no extremes of wet or dry. Bronze fennel requires little grooming, produces an effective showing over an extended season, and isn't insect- or disease-prone. Its anise-flavored leaves have a multitude of uses in the kitchen.

HUMULUS LUPULUS 'AUREUS'

Humulus lupulus, the source of commercial hops, is the single most important "worker" in the production of one of the world's most consumed beverages, beer. Perhaps not so curiously, the genus belongs to the Hemp Family, along with *Cannabis*, or marijuana. It is the golden-leaved *H. l.* 'Aureus' that is of interest to the adventurous gardener, strictly for its application as a decorative, living garden drapery. Its vines are root-hardy to below 0°F., and useful as well in mild climates where some light freezing occurs, but summers can be quite hot. This is one of those fast-growing vines that can be used to camouflage or obscure such necessities as the compost pile, the area where household waste is sorted and collected, or a garden toolshed that is less than picturesque. But golden-leaved hop vine is also a glowing yellow green that never looks better than when backlighted, the effect best observed while standing or sitting inside a trellis structure it has been encouraged to cover.

Propagate new vines from cuttings of the underground roots, taken in early spring when the winter-killed tops are removed to make way for this year's growth. Side-dressing with rotted manure in winter will result in the plants making exuberant progress the following season. Abundant ground moisture in spring encourages deep rooting and hop vines that can endure drier summer conditions.

BEES LOVE THE FRAGRANT HERB,
DRACOCEPHALUM MOLDAVICA (opposite far left).
BRONZE FENNEL AND ORANGE DARWIN TULIPS
PAIR SYNERGISTICALLY AT BARNSLEY HOUSE
(opposite near left). GOLDEN HOP VINE, *HUMULUS
LUPULUS* 'AUREUS' (right) SHADES THE CHAIR IN
ROSEMARY VEREY'S KITCHEN GARDEN.

LAVANDULA STOECHAS

English lavender, *Lavandula angustifolia*, is one of the most be-loved herbs of all time, for its clean scent that somehow man-ages to be at once both bracing and calming. There is also the delightful appearance of the plants in bloom and their habit of spilling out of prim hedges onto the garden pathway or over the side of a retaining wall. Oil of lavender is distilled from this species and the much less cultivated *L. stoechas*, known vari-ously as Spanish and French lavender. *Lavandula stoechas*, which can become a shrublet to three feet but is more often a third this size, produces downy, silvery gray leaves, and flower spikes that are formed into a distinctively squared bract, the upper two inches of which are rose-purple and long-lasting, and be-low which the small, dark purple flowers are borne in late spring and early summer. All parts of the plant are aromatic.

Perhaps what keeps *L. stoechas* from being commonplace, at least in the United States, is its tenderness to cold; a winter low of around 20°F. is about the limit. In colder regions it must be treated as an indoor/outdoor container plant that is wintered over in a sunny, cool, but essentially frost-free space such as an enclosed porch, or possibly a cold frame or green-house where hardy bonsai are wintered. Writer Ann Lovejoy describes the *L. stoechas* plants in her Washington garden in winter as having an architectural quality, with their whorls of narrow gray leaves. Somehow that description applies as well to this lavender in any other season and almost any other con-text that can be conjured. The plant in the photograph was blooming in early spring in a sun-heated pit greenhouse at Logee's Greenhouses in Connecticut, where the pot had been placed the previous autumn before hard frost. Propagate laven-der by soft- or hardwood cuttings taken in late summer or early autumn.

LEONURUS

Leonotis leonurus or lion's-ear, named for the heart-shaped leaves coated with very short hair, is a South African medicinal herb classed as a tender shrub, and growing to six or seven feet tall. The plant bears large numbers of tubular orange flowers, each to over two inches long and covered with scarlet hairs, along the upper quarter or so of every stalk. I once saw a magnificent row of these blooming in autumn at Taylor's Herb Gardens in Vista, California, a short distance north of San Diego. At colder, more northerly latitudes leonotis has the unfortunate habit of not reaching the blooming stage before it is cut down by frost. However, gardeners in temperate climes can grow the plant in a large container that is moved outdoors in warm weather to accent an herb, kitchen, or cottage garden. Like many of its relatives in the Mint Family, leonotis needs no staking if it receives full sun and ample breezes that shake the stems and cause them to become sturdy and self-reliant. However, container specimens that must be moved to warmer quarters at the onset of cold weather will probably need three or four cane stakes and twine ties to keep them at attention through the late autumn to early winter flowering season. Lion's-ear is eminently suited to Xeriscapes in the drier frost-free regions of the United States, and can play a role in herbaceous borders and cottage gardens where such temperate-climate favorites as peony and summer phlox cannot be grown because of insufficient winter cold.

FRENCH LAVENDER, *LAVANDULA STOECHAS*, HERE WITH GREEN-AND-WHITE EUONYMUS AT THE CHELSEA FLOWER SHOW, HAS LARGE SHOWY PURPLE BRACTS FROM WHICH ARE BORNE THE FRAGRANT, DARK PURPLE FLOWERS.

NEPETA MUSSINII

Catmint, *Nepeta mussinii* (not to be confused with catnip, *N. cataria*), is placed by traditionalists in the herb garden. But adventurous gardeners have appropriated it for herbaceous borders and cottage gardens, and now it's hard to decide whether to look for it among the herbs or the perennials. Catmint has a lot going for it, starting with cold-hardiness across all but the southernmost United States. Besides full sun and well-drained soil, this plant needs only a little moisture to help it get established, then its drought-tolerance can be counted upon. Small divisions removed and planted in the spring become large clumps themselves that need dividing possibly in their third spring, definitely in the fourth. This expansive habit leads to banks and path edgings of catmint. Two favorite ways to use catmint are to let it spill onto a garden pathway, or as a low, billowy softener for the front of a herbaceous border. Not only is the low, aromatic gray-green foliage attractive, but the lavender-blue flowers in midspring and summer are beautiful alone or in combinations of cool, hot, or mixed colors.

Catmint is considered a sweet herb that may be used as a tea. Cats love the plant, which fortunately has the grit to withstand their adorations.

Nepeta × *faassenii*, once known as *N. pseudomussinii*, is a sterile hybrid readily confused with *N. mussinii*. It grows to two feet and has violet-blue flowers in spring to summer.

A related plant, *Glechoma hederacea*, also called ground-ivy, Gill-over-the-ground, runaway Robin, field balm, or alehoof, was formerly included in the genus *Nepeta*. Ground-ivy is a creeping perennial used as a ground cover and sometimes naturalized, in which case it may be relegated to the lowly status of "weed". It needs less sun and more moisture than catmint and is attractive, especially in the horticultural form having variegated leaves, spilling from a hanging container or shelf.

CATMINT, RED VALERIAN, THISTLE, AND *SALVIA* 'EAST FRIESLAND' (DARK BLUE-PURPLE SPIKES) GROW AT THE NEW YORK BOTANICAL GARDEN.

OCIMUM BASILICUM

The introduction in the late 1950s of *Ocimum basilicum* 'Dark Opal', an All America Selections winner developed at the University of Connecticut, presaged such gardening trends as growing herbs in general and basils in particular, and an appreciation of edible plants as inherently beautiful. 'Dark Opal', from *O. basilicum* 'Purpurascens', may have been the first purple-leaved basil to hit the market, but the genes for purple are scattered through the genus. *Ocimum basilicum* 'Purple Ruffles', a recent AAS award winner, is large and vigorous, with deeply quilted leaves.

Today many gardeners grow basil just to have enough fresh leaves to appease their craving for pesto sauce. Consider also that for hundreds of years herbalists have promoted basil for relief of upper respiratory symptoms. Perhaps the growing awareness of air pollution is also part of the reason why basil has become so prevalent in American gardens.

Today this herb can be had in a multiplicity of forms and flavors. The traditional sweet basil is *O. basilicum*. 'Picollo' or 'Piccolo Fino Verde', a variant having smaller leaves, is said to be the original pesto basil. Lemon basil is *O. americanum*, a natural hybrid between *O. canum* of Kenya and South Africa and *O. b.* 'Purpurascens' of northwestern India. Thrysiflora basil, *O. b.* 'Thrysiflora', from India or Pakistan, is grown for the pyramidal purple flowers, which are distinctive both in the garden and when cut. Licorice basil, *O. b.* 'Anise Scented', from India, Pakistan, and possibly Thailand, has purplish overtones in the leaf veins, the florets, and the calyces, and an anise taste. Cinnamon basil, *O. b.* 'Cinnamon', from Northern India or possibly from European breeding, becomes covered with lavender flower spikes and tastes of cinnamon with a hint of cloves. 'Dwarf Bush' is best for growing indoors in a sunny window or under fluorescent lights.

MEXICAN BASIL (above) GIVES A THRILLING
PERFORMANCE IN THE GARDEN OR WHEN CUT.
PURPLE-FLECKED GREEN BASIL (below) IS BACKED BY
THE LARGER, AWARD-WINNING 'PURPLE RUFFLES'.

PERILLA FRUTESCENS

Perilla, the *shiso* of oriental cuisine, bears a strong resemblance to certain of the basils, particularly the recently introduced 'Purple Ruffles'. The shape of the quilted, purple-bronze leaves and their arrangement on the plant also suggest another relative, the coleus. The resemblance to the true basils is more than coincidental: *Perilla frutescens* was once known as *Ocimum frutescens*. 'Atropurpurea' (dark purple leaves) and 'Crispa' (leaves fringed, frilled, and wrinkled; often sold under the name *P. nankinensis*) are seen principally in cultivation. Less colorful forms have naturalized and may even be considered weeds under certain circumstances. However, once the desirable perillas are established from seeds sown where they are to grow, they will in succeeding seasons return by self-sowing. In this case, however, "weed" is hardly an apt description, for the gardener simply nurtures choice seedlings and rogues out the others while they are too small to offer any resistance. Sow the seeds when tomatoes are planted out into the garden. Perilla leaves reach their peak color in late summer.

POLYGONUM ODORATUM

Polygonum odoratum is a small and tidy species known variously as Vietnamese-mint and false coriander. The latter name refers to the taste and smell of the leaves which are just like those of the leaves of true coriander, popularly known as cilantro or Chinese parsley. The great value of false coriander for cooks is that it is in peak form in the summer while cilantro is more likely to be available for harvest earlier or later when the weather is cooler. The plant thrives in full sun and enriched garden loam that is irrigated weekly in hot, dry summer weather. It is carried over from one season to another by potting up and cutting back stock plants before frost. Cuttings are taken from the plants in late winter or early spring, and set out in the garden when the weather settles. Vietnamese-mint mixes well with a dwarf red barberry hedge in the herb garden at the Brooklyn Botanic Garden.

BOTH THE FENNEL AND PERILLA (left) AND THE VIETNAMESE-MINT (right) WERE PHOTOGRAPHED AT THE BROOKLYN BOTANIC GARDEN.

SESAMUM

Sesamum indicum, the source of commercial sesame seeds, thrives on long, hot summers and makes an annual flowering plant attractive enough for any cottage or kitchen garden. It reaches two to three feet in height, with bright green lance-shaped leaves up to five inches long. The one-inch, slipper-shaped flowers resemble those of foxglove and slipper gloxinia, and may be white or pale pink. They are followed by the inch-long capsules that when ripe are filled with sesame seeds ready to be toasted and eaten. The sesame plants I have seen most recently were growing under shade cloth in the trials conducted by the Park Seed Company in South Carolina, in the company of impatiens, begonias, salvias, and coleus, which suggests that in the hottest climates a partly shaded garden could be just right. But a long season of heat is essential in order for sesame to flower and ripen seeds. In the southernmost United States it has become naturalized, while in the coldest climates some gardeners grow sesame in large pots that can be moved to a warm greenhouse before the first frost.

SOLANUM MELONGENA

Solanum melongena 'Esculentum' gives us the everyday commercial eggplant, which forms following pollination of the star-shaped, two-inch violet flower. Botanically the plant is a spiny herb or small shrub from Africa and Asia, treated in North America as a warm-season annual, the same as its relatives, pepper, tomato, and potato. I have a hunch that certain gardeners appreciate the Nightshade Family as a whole, and perhaps they even will be adventurous enough to include some of the edible eggplants in the flower garden instead of relegating them to the vegetable or kitchen garden. The decorative eggplants I have in mind include the Oriental cultivars such as 'Pingtung Long', 'Chinese Long', 'Ichiban Hybrid', 'Orient Express', and 'Taiwan Long'. 'Pingtung Long' in particular is more colorful than the conventional dark purple eggplants. This variety is a bright lavender-purple hue that can be seen at some distance. The fruits, growing to 10 or 11 inches long and an inch and a half in diameter, also appear in clusters, and the overall effect in any garden can be remarkable. When up to a couple of inches long these eggplants can be harvested and stir-fried whole as tender baby vegetables.

The plants grow sturdily to two feet and are probably at their best in raised planting beds, so that the show of fruits can be more readily observed. Planting in hanging baskets, one plant to a 10-inch container, is another possibility for showing off the handsome fruits to best advantage. Oriental eggplant is attractive planted in a basket with 'Pink Cascade' petunias. Or grow it with yellow flowers, or any other color flower or foliage that is pleasing to the eye. Eggplant needs full sun, moist, well-drained soil, and constant warmth to grow well.

TAGETES LUCIDA

Pericon is another name for *Tagetes lucida*, a member of the same South American genus as the common marigolds with which almost every gardener is familiar. When *T. lucida* blooms, a close look reveals that the flowers are indeed small, single marigolds, gathered in clusters at the ends of the stems. The leaves are ferny or pinnate like those of common marigolds, and taste amazingly like true French tarragon. Pericon is being used increasingly in the culinary arts as a substitute for tarragon, which is at best difficult to force indoors in winter. Since both pericon and tarragon, *Artemisia dracunculus*, are in the Composite or Daisy Family, it is more understandable, although nonetheless remarkable, that they should contain essential oils having the same smell and taste. Since pericon is from the southern part of Oaxaca, Mexico, about 15 degrees north of the equator, it grows best when days are a little longer than nights. Plants may tend to languish or grow spindly indoors in far northern places during the shortest days of autumn and early winter, but one or two select plants can be brought along in a warm, fluorescent-light indoor garden. (Make one by mounting four 40-watt tubes 18 inches above a bench measuring four feet long and up to two feet wide.) Burn the lights 16 to 18 hours a day, maintain temperatures between 60° and 75°F., and operate a small fan to ensure that the air circulates freely, and the plant will think it is growing outdoors in the long days of summer. Both the flowers and leaves of pericon are edible. The flowers are a delightful addition to mixed green salads; the leaves can be used raw or cooked in the same fashion as true tarragon, or made into tea to treat colic or just to enjoy.

POPCORN 'PRETTY POPS', AT THE PARK SEED COMPANY IN SOUTH CAROLINA, MAY HAVE MULTICOLORED KERNELS. BUT THE POPCORN WILL BE ALL WHITE.

ZEA MAYS

Maize to most Americans is Kafir-corn, *Sorghum vulgare caffrorum*, so it may come as a surprise to learn that the species name for sweet corn is *mays*, although it is from another genus, *Zea*. Both genera belong to the Grass Family, the zeas from tropical America, the sorghums from Africa and the Mediterranean area. Almost any species from either group might be introduced as an ornamental grass into the cultivated border — excepting that rigorously root-hardy scourge of Southern farmers, Johnsongrass, *S. halepense*. Here we will consider only one variety of *Zea mays*, 'everta', or popcorn.

Look through books and seed catalogues to learn about either popcorn or so-called "decorative" or "ornamental" corn, and you will discover that one catalogue's popcorn, 'Strawberry' for example, is another's ornamental to enjoy for autumn door, table, and wreath arrangements. The catalogue of Shepherd's Garden Seeds recommends both uses for strawberry corn, calling it a dual-purpose plant. Shepherd's also notes that the variety is an heirloom that has been grown for generations. Most catalogue listings for Indian, rainbow, or calico corn, in various sizes from "mini" ears on dwarf stalks to large ears that appear on plants "as high as an elephant's eye," note only that these varieties are for hanging on your door as a harvest symbol. But some of them are in fact excellent for popping, others for drying and grinding into flour or meal.

Hardly any other plant in this book has the ability to make its presence known so rapidly when sown in hills spaced proportionately through an herbaceous border or cottage garden. Mature corn grows from seed in three months. For a more dramatic effect in the garden, pull back the husks as the ears become ripe, to expose the colorful kernels.

CHAPTER
FOUR

RARE
BULBS

In this chapter I will consider bulbs broadly, to include true bulbs, corms, tubers, rhizomes, fleshy roots, and one plant that definitely isn't a bulb but is so universally marketed with them that this seems the logical place for its introduction. Most if not all of the bulbs here are meant to be kept, not discarded after the first season of bloom. Not all of them disappear from aboveground for a season every year, but they do have in common the ability to store moisture and a need for an annual period of semidormancy. The annual disappearance of 'bulb' plants — especially rare and endangered ones — may help to preserve their wild populations; even the most experienced plant hunters can be thwarted in collecting a bulb from underground when there is no evidence of it above. The vanishing act is also part of what makes bulbs so endlessly fascinating to gardeners. ❧ Bulbs are in a special position today, due to recent legislation designed to stop the decimation of native stands and to encourage the propagation of endangered species by professional growers, the same as the more familiar garden bulbs. Because of this law, unusual bulbs, when offered, will be of high quality commercial stock, rather than specimens taken from the wild. Demand is sure to grow, and will lead to a wider range of choices for gardeners. The opening up of the world to free trade will further increase traffic in bulbs. Allen Lacy notes in his introduction to a 1990 reissue of Louise Beebe Wilder's classic book, Adventures with Hardy Bulbs (originally published in 1936), that during the First and Second World Wars, a plant quarantine curtailed bulb imports from overseas, and it was extremely difficult for American gardeners to obtain many rare and desirable species. In recent years the supply of South African bulbs has been similarly cut, as a result of the problems in that country. Gardeners are hoping for a restoration of stability in South Africa that will again permit a free horticultural relationship with this source of truly incredible bulbs — and other flora as well. ❧ One of the most appealing South African bulbs for pot or garden culture is Cyrtanthus. It is treated much like the florist amaryllis, and deserves to be more widely cultivated. It responds enthusiastically to container growing and flowers naturally in winter or spring, thrilling the nose as well as the eye. ❧ Gardeners are planting bulbs both rare and common with perennials, and learning to appreciate a flowerbed filled with different colors, textures, shapes, and plants in various stages of growth. On a stroll through writer Katherine Whiteside's garden she remarked that daffodil leaves can be pretty as a textural element in a garden, which, after all, is not just about flowers. She also believes that gardeners are learning to appreciate the smaller bulbs, such as species tulips. Gardeners now are willing to plant these small, quiet bulbs and wait for them to establish colonies. Such naturalized plantings will grow bigger and better with the passage of seasons, Whiteside believes, while flashier, more commercial bulbs will eventually fade away. ❧ In addition to the bulbous plants covered in this chapter, one might also like to consider growing the eight-foot eremurus or desert candle, the Moroccan hoop-petticoat daffodil from the Atlas Mountains, and hosts of species iris and lilies.

'LILAC WONDER' IS A MIDSEASON CULTIVAR OF *TULIPA BAKERI* (shown on previous pages with broom, *CYTISUS × PRAECOX*), A SPECIES NATIVE TO CRETE ALSO KNOWN AS *T. SAXATILIS* OR CLIFF TULIP. *IRIS* 'SHELFORD GIANT' TAKES THE STAGE IN LATE SPRING (above) WITH RAMBLER ROSES AT RIVER FARM, THE VIRGINIA HEADQUARTERS OF THE AMERICAN HORTICULTURAL SOCIETY.

ACIDANTHERA

Acidanthera is an Ethiopian genus of the Iris Family that can be wintered over outdoors only in the warmest climates. Elsewhere the corms are treated like gladiolus, planted when danger of frost has passed, in clumps of ten or so, four to six inches apart and as deep, in clayey soil. The fans of sword-shaped leaves are smaller and more graceful than those of the familiar garden glads. In mid- to late summer the flowering spikes, each carrying as many as six blossoms, break from the leaves and when open, perfume the air, revealing the reason for the name, fragrant gladiolus. In autumn, before frost, as the leaves begin to wither, dig, clean, and store the corms in a cool, dark place.

One species, *Acidanthera bicolor*, is in cultivation; a variant, *Murieliae*, differs by having flattened corms more like those of *Gladiolus*, the genus in which this plant was previously included. Acidantheras are included in the fragrance garden at Brooklyn Botanic Garden, where the raised planting beds lift the blossoms to nose level. They are a big hit every year, for both the blossoms that hover like white butterflies with reddish-brown blotches, and their refreshing scent.

ALLIUM

The genus *Allium* contains four hundred different rhizomatous or bulbous herbs from the Northern Hemisphere. Some of them can become weeds if they are permitted to self-sow. Chives, *A. schoenoprasum*, are perhaps the most widely cultivated of the alliums. They are cold-hardy throughout the continental United States and thrive in any sunny, well-drained site. They multiply generously from seeds and divisions.

The obviously ornamental onions can be choice plants for borders, cottage, rock, and wild gardens. Ornamental alliums belong in cutting gardens, too — the flowerheads are freely borne and in some cases, sweet-scented. They also last well when cut, and dry nicely if left to stand in a vase. Globular clusters of white, yellow, pink, red, blue, or purple flowers occur at the tops of bare stalks taller than the leaves. *Allium giganteum*, the giant onion of the cut flower trade, is almost a cliché. I prefer the smaller, starrier blossoms of such species as Turkestan onion, *A. karataviense.* The plant has a many-flowered umbel in mid spring and broad, flat leaves, 10 inches long and up to five inches wide, that make a handsome show on bare ground. Golden garlic, *A. moly*, is a hardier plant that grows a foot tall, with gray-green leaves an inch wide and a multitude of yellow flowers in loose heads in late spring. It naturalizes and can tolerate some shade. *Allium cyaneum* has grassy leaves in a dense clump to 10 inches high, and rising above it clusters of bright blue, gracefully nodding flowers. This species is an excellent choice for a rock garden, or near the front of a border, as well as in cut flower arrangements.

ACIDANTHERA (opposite) BRINGS BUTTERFLIES TO LATE SUMMER GARDENS. *BEGONIA GRANDIS* (above) BLOOMS IN AUTUMN AT RIVER FARM IN VIRGINIA.

BEGONIA GRANDIS

That a begonia could be winter-hardy to 0°F. comes as a shock to gardeners familiar only with summer bedding begonias and seasonal flowering potted Riegers. The hardy begonia, *Begonia grandis* (formerly known as *B. evansiana*), which produces bulbils in the leaf axils that fall to the ground in autumn and grow to flowering size late the following summer, has orange-reddish stems and angel-wing leaves that are olive green with red veins and red hairs. The generous, drooping cymes of male and female flowers — rosy pink in the species, white in the cultivar 'Alba' — begin in midsummer and continue until killing frost. The maturing seed capsules are also pink. Hardy begonia does well in humusy, well-drained soil supplied with moisture in the summer. It is the perfect lodger for a cottage or perennial flower garden in half shade, although the plants in full bloom never look lovelier than when back- or cross-lighted by direct sun, especially early or late in the day.

CAMASSIA

The camassias are graceful, bulbous plants from the Lily Family, native to the Pacific Northwest. A cluster of long, narrow, tapering leaves grows from the bulb, with the flower stalk rising from the center in late spring. The starry flowers, with their long, narrow, widely separated petals, are mostly blue or lavender, but can also be white or pale yellow. Camassias are underutilized plants for late-spring bloom in the border or wild garden and can be especially effective at the edge of a pond or bog. Plant camassias in autumn, four inches deep,

nine inches apart, in sandy, well-drained loam in a sunny spot. They do best when the soil is dry in summer, moist at other times. Winter flooding is ideal for them.

Cultivars of *Camassia leichtlinii* are much sought-after for their fortuitous timing: they flower in the quiet time, after the main wash of spring bloom and before the bounty of summer. There is a blue-purple cultivar seen in some of England's finest gardens. But these plants deserve to be far more widely grown in the United States. I have recently seen a blue camassia beginning to colonize in a garden in the Northeast, which proves that they will grow outside of cool, moist climates like those of England and the Pacific Northwest.

CORYDALIS LUTEA

This spring-flowering, all-but-indestructible species from southern Europe is not in any sense a true bulb or for that matter a tuber, corm, or rhizome. But it does have thickened roots (when crushed they give off a nitrogenous odor), and I have included it in this category because most suppliers sell the divisions along with bulbs such as tulips and daffodils for autumn planting. *Corydalis lutea* is a hardy perennial for Zones 5 to 8 that is mostly evergreen but is often treated as an annual, possibly because the roots have been purchased along with other bulbs that are treated as expendable after the first season of bloom. The flowers resemble those of fringed bleeding-heart, but are yellow with a short spur. The graceful plant grows about 15 inches high, with feathery, finely divided leaves that are green on top and glaucous (covered with whitish powder) on the underside, giving the impression when a breeze ripples through that they are blue-green. Corydalis is attractive in the open border or the wild garden; it is especially lovely along a rock garden path or spilling from a dry rock wall.

One of the most remarkable colonies I have seen of *C. lutea* was in just such a sunny wall in northwestern Connecticut at the H. Lincoln Foster garden. An heirloom brown and yellow German iris grew up from the base of the wall, and the yellow beards of its flowers resonated with the color of the corydalis. Less a folk plant and more a connoisseur's is the white-flowered *C. l.* 'Alba', which is the same as the species in every way except for color. *Corydalis aurea*, an American native annual or biennial, grows to six inches, with bright green leaves and yellow flowers all summer. There are numerous other species, some having flowers in shades of pink, rose, yellow, or blue. Give corydalis partial shade or full sun, a light, porous soil, and moderate moisture. Propagate new plants from seed or by division of the rootstock.

CRINUM

Crinum belongs to the Amaryllis Family and grows wild in many places in the tropical and warm-temperate regions of both hemispheres. The sword-shaped to strap-like leaves, mostly spirally arranged, can be several feet long and up to five inches wide. Crinums bloom in spring and summer. Lots of space is a prerequisite for growing them, which explains why they are seldom seen as container plants. They are extremely popular outdoor plants in the Deep South — so popular, in fact, that they are called ditch lilies. Some crinums are ev-

ergreen, others die back to the ground in autumn. In regions where temperatures drop below 10°F. in winter, crinums must be dug in autumn. Plant evergreen species in pots and keep them semidormant, watering only very occasionally.

The milk-and-wine lily, *C. latifolium zeylanicum*, grows from an eight-inch, short-necked bulb. Its white Easter-lily-like trumpet flowers have wine red markings, as do those of *C. sanderanum*, another milk-and-wine lily. In the South, crinums often remain undisturbed for several generations in gardens, where they colonize and provide a spectacular show. To the uninitiated, bringing into cultivation any crinum, ditch lily or not, is an adventure.

CROCOSMIA

Crocosmia 'Lucifer' was recently shown on the cover of the Royal Horticultural Society's magazine *The Garden*, its screaming scarlet flowers in the company of the religiously scarlet dahlia 'Bishop of Llandaff' and a purple-leaved cordyline. It was a daring but entirely satisfactory use of 'Lucifer', a super-strong cultivar that has taken by storm the cognoscenti of

The plants quickly colonize, sending up their grassy, bright green leaves each spring. In mid- to late summer the plants become vibrant patches of green and red, about three feet high. The blossoms, borne on wiry stems freesia-style, last up to a month in the garden and for a week when cut. The photo here shows 'Lucifer' in the Pennsylvania garden of Sir John

herbaceous borders. Gertrude Jekyll would surely place this flower, as well as the dark yellow cultivar 'Jenny Bloom', with the hot colors. *Crocosmia* as a genus has been around, sometimes going by the name of *Montbretia*. But it is this upstart 'Lucifer' that makes adventurous gardeners think anew about growing Crocosmia. According to plantsman John Elsley this cultivar's strength and extra hardiness can be attributed to its parentage; it is the progeny of a mating between Crocosmia and another South African genus of irids, *Curtonus*.

Thouron, in July, accompanied by the burnished burgundy bracts of acanthus. With a heavy winter mulch crocosmia can withstand temperatures to below 0°F. and will grow so thickly it will require division in only three or four years.

If crocosmia is appealing, seek out others besides 'Lucifer'. The hybrid species × *crocosmiiflora* grows to four feet, with orange to crimson flowers; 'Aurantiaca' is dark orange; *masoniorum*, orange-scarlet; and 'Citronella', with large flowers of clear yellow, is similar to 'Jenny Bloom'.

FRITILLARIA

The crown imperial, *Fritillaria imperialis*, is one of the most extraordinary looking plants of spring. Never mind that the leaves smell of skunk, this member of the Lily Family commands attention from the time it breaks through the soil in early spring until the brick red, upside-down "tulip" flowers topped with pineapple-style green bracts start to fade. (Then one will be thinking of ways to camouflage the increasingly tattered-looking leaves and stalks, which must stand until their work of storing energy for another season is complete, in early summer.) The bulbs grow to six inches in diameter and the plants may rise to four or five feet.

Crown imperial, for all its aristocratic bearing, is common, but not the cultivars which have yellow flowers, and which are also less tolerant of cold. Rarest of all are the selections of imperialis having white-striped leaves. Such variegated forms have appeared spontaneously in plantings as long as fritillaries have been cultivated. Crown imperials made their way into gardens after bulbs were collected in northern India, Afghanistan, and Iran. Another popular fritillaria, the guinea-hen flower or checkered lily, *F. meleagris*, also blooms in spring, its solitary bell flowers pinkish purple or white prominently checkered, nodding on slender stems above narrow, grassy leaves. This species has naturalized over vast parts of Europe and England and is extremely hardy. Many other species also await adventuring gardeners, including: *F. camschatcensis*, with dark blackish purple or brown flowers; *F. cirrhosa*, purple or yellowish green with dark purple checkered patterns; *F. pallidiflora*, a robust plant having broadly lance-shaped, gray-green leaves scattered pleasingly along the stems, topped by yellow to greenish yellow flowers faintly checked in brownish red within; and *F. persica*, to four feet, with brownish purple-black bells. It is a challenge to situate the tall fritillaries to best show off their beauty.

RARE *FRITILLARIA IMPERIALIS* 'VARIEGATA' (above)
BLOOMS IN EARLY SPRING AT HORTUS BULBORUM
IN THE NETHERLANDS.

SUMMER HYACINTH (below), *GALTONIA CANDICANS*, WAS PHOTOGRAPHED IN LATE SUMMER AT THE STRYBING ARBORETUM IN SAN FRANCISCO. IT HAS RECENTLY PROVED HIGHLY SUCCESSFUL IN GARDENS AT BATTERY PARK CITY IN NEW YORK. THE FRAGRANT FLOWERS APPEAR OVER A LONG SEASON AND ARE ALSO CHOICE FOR FRESH ARRANGEMENTS.

GLADIOLUS ITALICUS (opposite), OR *G. SEGETUM*, IS THE SPRING-FLOWERING CORN FLAG OR SWORD LILY OF SOUTHERN GARDENS. IT IS SEEN HERE IN BLOOM IN LATE APRIL INTERLACING AN OLD WROUGHT IRON FENCE AT JASMINE HILL IN ALABAMA, A FASCINATING AND BEAUTIFUL FORMERLY PRIVATE GARDEN NOW OPEN TO THE PUBLIC.

GALTONIA

Summer hyacinth, *Galtonia candicans*, is a member of the Lily Family and was once known as *Hyacinthus candicans*. Since the stout scape rises two to four feet tall, the reference to hyacinth may have more to do with scent than appearance. Galtonia is blessed by blooming relatively late, when the garden stage is uncrowded. Strap-shaped leaves grow to as much as three feet long and two inches wide. The fragrant flowers, each to nearly two inches, are pure white, and they appear over a long season from midsummer to autumn. Lovers of pale green flowers can grow *G. viridiflora*. Give galtonia rich, moist soil, and half to full sun. In northern regions lift and store the bulbs in autumn like gladiolus. On an early autumn tour of the plantings installed in recent times at Battery Park City, a landfill developed on the lower west side of Manhattan in New York City, horticulturist Timothy Steinhoff singled out galtonia as having proved itself an outstanding urban plant. It is botanically a bulbous, perennial herb, native to South Africa, that can be propagated from offsets or seeds and is considered best suited to mild and warm climates.

Galtonia is sold with the other summer-flowering bulbs — dahlia, gladiolus, and canna. The plants make handsome clumps in borders and in mild climates a colony may well stand on its own, especially if set so as to give the white blossoms a flattering background such as yew or boxwood. Galtonias make splendid cut flowers that will probably be mistaken for Mexican tuberoses, *Polianthes tuberosa*. Curiously enough, the tuberose belongs to the allied Agave Family, so the two plants are approximately kissing cousins, although galtonia can probably tolerate temperatures about ten degrees colder. The flowers of the Mexican tuberose are creamy, velvety white while those of galtonia are more, as Penelope Hobhouse says, "laundry white".

GLADIOLUS

I once knew a woman in the decorative arts who uttered "gladiola" as a curse. Surely she had never seen the small and graceful wild forms of *Gladiolus*, sometimes called corn flag or sword lily, a genus containing upwards of three hundred species from tropical and South Africa, Europe, the Mediterranean, and Near East. *Gladiolus italicum*, also listed as *G. segetum*, from the Mediterranean region to Turkestan and Iran, has naturalized in warmer parts of the United States. I have seen it in late April all across Alabama, Mississippi, and Louisiana. The loose spike of up to 20 bright, pinkish purple, two-inch flowers grows to three feet and appears variously in mid- to late spring in Zone 8 and south. *Gladiolus tristis*, from South Africa, sends up in winter three slender leaves to 18 inches, followed by spring flowers of fragrant cream to white, with purple keels. Pots of this species have won blue ribbons at the Philadelphia Flower Show. It can be grown in a sun-heated pit or a regular greenhouse having cool to moderate night temperatures in winter, with full sun and free air movement by day. Even so, *G. tristis* when potted will need cane stakes and deft tying to hold it upright. 'Christabel' is a spring-flowering hybrid having similar cold hardiness, with wiry stems topped by a loose spike of fragrant, funnel-shaped, primrose yellow flowers with purple-brown veining in the upper petals. Its garden appearance is more like that of the related *Acidanthera* than the stubbornly tall and stiff commercial gladiolus.

Not all species of gladiolus bloom in the spring. There are those that bloom in summer and autumn as well; I have seen gladiolus flowering in early autumn at Descanso Gardens in California. Dealers in rare bulbs sell corms of species *Gladiolus*, and one may find seeds listed, although only rarely.

HIPPEASTRUM

Northern gardeners accustomed to the large-flowered Dutch amaryllis sold in pots for holiday or winter bloom are often surprised and always delighted to find that smaller, somehow more fascinating species in the same genus are grown outdoors all year in mild climates. The graceful evergreen leaves of some species persist through winter and the flowers appear on schedule each spring, often at Easter; to West Indian gardeners they are known as Easter lilies. The true *Amaryllis belladonna* is from South Africa but the plants grown as amaryllis are mostly members of the genus *Hippeastrum*, only one of which is found in western Africa; the rest are from tropical America.

Hippeastrum puniceum, with bright green leaves to two inches wide, produces new leaves following its spring blooms, umbels of two to four bright red flowers with green bases. Stands of these left undisturbed in warm climates can become impressive colonies with hundreds of blooms. They can also be potted in clay bulb pans or azalea pots 10 inches in diameter and left for many years, until the pot is nearly bursting with roots. While the commercial amaryllis is routinely sold already potted in a peat-based medium, they grow best in a mixture of fibrous loam, leaf mold, and sand that has a neutral or slightly alkaline pH. Grow the plant from divisions or from seeds, which will produce blooming plants after two or three seasons. 'Semiplenum' is a semidouble collectible.

LACHENALIA

LACHENALIA ALOIDES (above), A SPECIES OF CAPE
COWSLIP, BELONGS TO THE LILY FAMILY. THE ONE
SHOWN HERE WAS BLOOMING IN MIDWINTER AT
KARTUZ GREENHOUSES IN CALIFORNIA, FROM A
SIX-INCH BULB PAN.

My first meeting with *Lachenalia* or Cape cowslip was near the end of February, in a small old greenhouse that once housed a collection of South African bulbs on the grounds at Long-wood Gardens in Pennsylvania. There *L. reflexa* was a thing of absolute beauty, with its glowing yellow, green-tinged tubular bell flowers, the basal leaves spotted and extending two or three inches beyond the rim of a five-inch clay pot, its flower-ing stalk standing six inches high. My next encounter was with *L. aloides* at Kartuz Greenhouses in Vista, California, again in February, but this species was a littler taller, with red-tipped bells of glowing apricot. Altogether there are upwards of fifty different species in this genus of bulbs belonging to the Lily Family, characterized by basal, often spotted, somewhat suc-culent leaves and terminal spikes or racemes of flowers that are mostly white, yellow, red, or lavender-blue.

Lachenalia can be grown outdoors in frost-free climates. Elsewhere, pot the bulbs in humus-rich loam in late summer or early autumn and place in a cold frame until the last weeks in November. Then move the pots to a greenhouse or other sunny, airy growing space with 50°F. nights and daytime tem-peratures only 10°F. or so warmer. After flowering, continue watering and fertilizing in a sunny, moderate to warm growing space until the foliage ripens, then keep the bulb dry and dark until time for repotting.

The flowers of *L. aloides* 'Quadricolor' are red at the base, greenish yellow in the middle, and tipped with green, red-purple inside. In late winter or early spring, *L. glaucina* bears generous quantities of fragrant bells, white with an almost otherworldly iridescent glow that may be blue, red, yellow, or green. Lachenalia bulbs are available from dealers who special-ize in bulbs, especially those from South Africa. The plants can also be propagated from seeds.

ORNITHOGALUM

Ornithogalum is a genus of hardy and tender bulbous plants in the Lily Family, from Africa and the Mediterranean. The plants are eminently suited to both pot and garden culture, depending on the species and the climate. The ornithogalum's claim to fame is the chincherinchee, *O. thyrsoides*, of commercial cut flower growers. It is cold-hardy to Zone 7 and can be grown like gladiolus or in pots for summer bloom in the North. The leaves, about a foot long and two inches wide, arise directly from the bulb. The white flowers are gathered in a dense raceme toward the top of an 18-inch stalk. There is also a yellow-flowered variety, 'Aureum'. *Ornithogalum arabicum*, a tender species, is similar in appearance except the white flowers have a noticeable black pistil. This one can have sinuously curving stems that are pure delight and an inspiration to interpretive flower arrangers. *Ornithogalum nutans*, hardy to Zone 6, has narrower leaves to 18 inches long and one half inch wide that ripen soon after the midspring flowering. The individual flowers, to two inches across, with white petals attractively edged in green, are in loose clusters on stalks to 18 inches. This species has been seen in the gardens at Sissinghurst and will no doubt be increasingly popular for some years to come. The most ubiquitous species of the family, *O. umbellatum*, is one of several plants called "star-of-Bethlehem". It grows a foot tall with green-edged white, starry flowers in spring.

To grow ornithogalum in pots, set bulbs close together in an all-purpose mix such as equal parts garden loam, well-rotted compost, and sand. Keep cool and moist until leaf growth begins, at which time full sun and cool night temperatures, below 50°F., are essential. It is vital to keep the leaves growing as long as possible after flowering so as to properly fatten up the bulbs for the coming year.

SCHIZOSTYLIS

Crimson-flag and Kaffir-lily are the common names for two South African species of *Schizostylis*, herbs from the Iris Family with fibrous, fleshy roots, that are seen rarely in North American gardens. I first encountered these unique flowers blooming in early autumn at the University of British Columbia Botanical Garden in Vancouver. There was the species *S. coccinea*, with erect sword-shaped leaves to 12 inches, reminiscent of gladiolus but more graceful, and a delightful abundance of crimson-red flowers to two inches across and to two feet tall. The Garden

SCHIZOSTYLIS COCCINEA (opposite upper), CRIMSON-FLAG OR KAFFIR-LILY, BLOOMS OVER A LONG SEASON BEGINNING IN EARLY AUTUMN. THE *FLEUR-DE-LIS* FLOWERS OF *SPREKELIA FORMOSISSIMA* (opposite lower) APPEAR SINGLY IN EARLY SUMMER ABOVE AMARYLLIS-LIKE LEAVES.

also had some promising seedlings, and cross-pollinated blossoms encased in special bags to keep insects from contaminating the breeder's work. Ann Lovejoy in *The Border in Bloom* calls schizostylis a trooper, and notes that two cultivars performed beautifully for her. She describes 'Sunrise' as "big, wide, and satin pink, looking like an overblown gladiola." 'Viscountess Byng', which is similar but smaller, blooms for Lovejoy " . . . from October through March." In colder climates, the gardener smitten with schizostylis can satisfy the craving by potting and growing the plant under glass for winter bloom and cut flowers. Later keep the soil on the dry side until new leaves start to grow in spring or early summer. Use a loam-based, all-purpose potting soil. Top-dress with fresh soil every year at the beginning of the growing season.

SPREKELIA

Sprekelia formosissima is a single-species genus belonging to the Amaryllis Family, often confused with a related but different plant, the *Hippeastrum*. *Sprekelia* is a bulbous herb from Mexico that can be cultivated outdoors in gardens from Zone 8 south. The bright crimson flowers to four inches diameter are borne singly on 12-inch stalks in spring or summer. The plant's common names, including Jacobean lily, St. James' lily, Aztec lily, and orchid amaryllis, are indicative of a popular folk plant. The names may also have been glamorized by catalogue writers attempting to make accessible and appealing a plant that is quite out of the ordinary. The linear leaves, to almost an inch wide and 12 inches tall, appear at the same time as the *fleur-de-lis*-shaped flowers. One of the nicest plantings I have seen was in a southern California garden where the sprekelia flowers and leaves stood out stunningly against a background of gray santolina hedging.

It is only fair to tell the "terrible truth" about sprekelia, that after the purchased bulb blooms the first time around it can be temperamental about blooming in succeeding seasons. One possible solution to this problem is to set the bulb in a five-inch clay pot — or several of the purchased bulbs in one 12-inch bulb pan — and leave them undisturbed until the roots are very crowded. Another is to situate the sprekelia so that it is subjected to considerable summer heat and sun with a little stressing from drying-out toward the end of the active growth period. Keep the pot frost-free but cool and on the dry side until spring, then top-dress with enriched potting soil, first removing an inch or two of the old soil mix. At the very least, water with liquid manure about the color of weak tea, when the conditions are dependably warm with lots of sun. (This treatment is effectual for most potted amaryllids.)

STERNBERGIA LUTEA (above) BLOOMS THROUGH AUTUMN, UNTIL FROST. MEXICAN SHELL FLOWER

TIGRIDIA (below) OPENS NEW BLOSSOMS DAILY IN HOT, SUNNY WEATHER.

STERNBERGIA

Five species of *Sternbergia* occur in southeastern Europe and southeastern Asia. They are bulbs from the Amaryllis Family that are garden-hardy in Zones 6 to 9. *Sternbergia* is ideally suited to planting in a dry, sunny location where the soil is both heavy and well-drained, a somewhat unlikely situation that can often be managed most readily in a rock garden. The most popular species is the winter daffodil, *S. lutea*, which is planted in late summer or early autumn, for bloom in about six weeks or ahead of hard frost. Plant the bulbs in September with the top of the long neck about one inch below the soil surface. They do best in full sun to half shade and spread slowly by offsets and seeds. The name winter daffodil (the plant is also called lily-of-the-field) is suggested by the leaves, which can be up to 12 inches long, and resemble those of the true daffodil. The leaves appear with or after the flowers and generally persist until the following spring. The flowers are more like those of the crocus than either a daffodil or lily.

There is a fine colony of winter daffodil in the rock garden at the Brooklyn Botanic Garden. It disappears in the spring when the majority of plants are just beginning and reappears later often as something of a surprise when the first blooms open. Sternbergia is one of those plants that tends to bloom well in alternate years, so if the yield was disappointing this autumn, take heart; the cycle holds greater promise next time around. The cultivar 'Major' has larger flowers than *S. lutea*. A spring-flowering species, *S. candida*, grows from basal, grayish green leaves; its fragrant, funnel-shaped white flower is quite like a crocus, and grows to two inches across. In climates too cold for *S. lutea* to stay in the garden it can be grown in a bulb pan and wintered in any frost-free growing space that is sunny and airy. A sun-heated pit is ideal; a cold frame or possibly a very cool greenhouse are other possibilities.

TIGRIDIA

Tiger flower, shell flower, and one-day lily are folk names for *Tigridia*, a member of the Iris Family with 27 species of bulbous, perennial herbs from temperate Mexico, Guatemala, and the Andes of Peru and Chile. *Tigridia pavonia*, from Mexico and Guatemala, has long, narrow, furrowed leaves beneath a flower stalk that grows to two feet high and from which the tripetaled flowers are borne fresh daily. The blossoms have a distinct, unique perianth that is red, spotted with yellow and purple in the cuplike center. Several cultivars are listed in catalogues by color: white, pink, yellow, purple, orange, and rose. Hardly any flower that lasts for only a day, including the most extraordinary of hybrid hemerocallis and Chinese hibiscus, is more spectacular than the tigridia. In addition to their obvious beauty, tigridias also have the refreshing habit of blooming reliably day after day, even in the hottest and sunniest of summer weather. Another amazing thing about the tigridia is that the bulbs are used as food in some areas where the wild plants are plentiful.

As garden plants tigridias are usually treated like gladiolus, except in Zone 8 and south, where they can be established in the garden in well-drained soil in a site that receives full sun in summer. Plant the bulbs two to three inches deep and six inches apart in soil that has been enhanced with well-rotted compost and possibly a light dusting of 5-10-10 fertilizer. Dig the bulbs before hard frost and store in a dry place without separating the clusters until replanting the following spring. If seeds can be obtained, plant them in sandy soil in flats; keep them moist, out of the sun, and at around 60°F. until they germinate. Plantlets develop tiny bulbs and may look frail, but after the last frost, set them outdoors where they are to grow. There may even be some flowers the first season — another amazing characteristic of tigridia.

TROPAEOLUM

Tropaeolum tricolorum, an herbaceous, climbing nasturtium whose delicate-appearing but strong stems arise from small tubers, blooms from early spring to early summer. In the United States it is seldom winter-hardy except in the warmest climates; elsewhere few plants are better suited for spending winter in a conservatory or a sun-heated pit. A temperature of 41°F. is about the minimum. I encountered this nasturtium on a May visit to Great Dixter in England, where a preeminent hor-

ticulturist and writer, Christopher Lloyd, is also foremost of the practicing gardeners. *Tropaeolum tricolorum* was in a grouping of container plants at the front door. Another species, *T. tuberosum*, seen in Pacific Northwest gardens as a sociable climber encouraged to interlace over any convenient hedge or shrub, is grown for its edible tubers in the high Andes. All parts of tropaeolum contain mustard oil, which explains why the young leaves, flowerbuds, freshly opened flowers, and even the seeds lend a peppery snap to green salads.

TULBAGHIA

Tulbaghia belongs to the Amaryllis Family, with up to two dozen distinct species found wild in tropical and southern Africa. They are classed variously as perennial, tuberous, or cormous herbs. Two species and a variety with variegated leaves are becoming more popular in Sun Belt gardens where temperatures generally do not fall below 20°F. They adapt readily to indoor/outdoor container management in colder regions. Plant in a light, sandy soil to encourage sturdy foliage and abundant flowering.

Tulbaghia fragrans has grassy leaves up to a foot long and

TULBAGHIA VIOLACEA GRACES A DOORYARD HERB GARDEN AT LIVE OAK GARDENS IN LOUISIANA. *TROPAEOLUM TRICOLORUM* (far left) BLOOMS AT GREAT DIXTER IN ENGLAND, WITH *GLADIOLUS TRISTIS* AND RED-AND-WHITE PARROT TULIP.

three-quarters of an inch wide. Umbels of 30 to 40 sweet-scented, bright lilac, half-inch-long flowers rise on gracefully curving, self-supporting stems to 18 inches tall. They are sweetly fragrant and appear intermittently all year. *Tulbaghia violacea* grows to 30 inches tall in bloom, with up to 20 flowers in each umbel. Each fragrant blossom is urn-shaped, three-quarters of an inch long, and bright lilac with a darker median stripe. The leaves become masses of handsome foliage 12 inches tall. When crushed, disturbed, or warmed just by the sun they smell rather acutely of garlic, accounting for the common name, society garlic. The tulbaghias respond to rainfall by flowering abundantly and producing new leaves, then retreat to semidormancy during dry or cold periods. Do not, however, let the bulbs dry completely.

TULIPA

New trade laws enacted to discourage the sale of bulbs collected from the wild and to promote their propagation under cultivation will have a far-ranging effect on the availability of species tulips, of which there may be well over a hundred. The complex hybrids with which we are familiar, the pictured 'Ice Follies' being a prime example, go back several hundred years and include most colors except true blue. All have arisen from bulbous, perennial herbs belonging to the Lily Family and native to temperate regions of the Old World and central Asia. "Perennial" is an important word here, for the hybrid tulips planted yearly by the billions are treated mainly as annuals. The species are more likely to perform as return-engagement perennials, in time forming colonies. *Tulipa tarda* (catalogues often list it as *T. dasystemon*), from Turkestan, with a veritable nosegay of white-tipped yellow flowers from flat-spreading leaves, to six inches, has colonized in one Connecticut garden I have seen, where it is among the last tulips of the spring season to bloom. By contrast, *T. biflora*, an Asian native, opens its starry cream, yellow, and pink flowers at the very dawn of spring; a dozen of these diminutive blossoms equals approximately the mass of a single hybrid 'Red Emperor'.

Give species tulips a site that receives full sun in spring and summer, with sharply drained soil that ideally is moist from autumn through spring, then drier in summer when the leaves have matured, withered, and disappeared. A rock garden is the perfect place, or plant them at the top of a retaining wall where they may be seen up close.

'ICE FOLLIES' TULIP (above) IS A MODERN MIDSEASON HYBRID, STOCKS OF WHICH ARE BEING MULTIPLIED IN THE NETHERLANDS. IT HAS ALREADY BEEN INTRODUCED TO THE HUNDREDS OF THOUSANDS OF VISITORS WHO ANNUALLY COME TO THE KEUKENHOF.

VELTHEIMIA

The genus *Veltheimia* includes five species of South African bulbs in the Lily Family. The two most widely cultivated, *V. capensis* and *V. viridifolia*, have rosettes of undulating lance-shaped leaves arising from the bulb and a stout scape 12 to 18 inches tall. On top is a raceme of small flowers resembling those of red-hot-poker but in cool combinations of pink, green, and purple. "Hippeastrum culture" is horticultural shorthand for the care they require, although the season of dormancy is different. Plant veltheimia bulbs in early autumn with the tips barely covered, outdoors in the ground in frost-free climates, elsewhere in a six- to eight-inch bulb pan. Use a loam-based, all-purpose potting soil (such as equal parts garden loam, sphagnum peat moss, sharp sand, and well-rotted compost). Keep indoors plants in any frost-free place. Temperatures throughout the autumn and winter are best in a cool to moderate range, up to about 60°F, combined with fresh air and as much direct sun as possible. The plants bloom from midwinter into spring, as average temperatures and daylength increase. At this time, water more and begin fertilizing with a flower-booster formula such as 15-30-15. When flowering ends, continue watering and fertilizing. Veltheimias need constantly increasing heat toward summer and then a period of gradual drying off until the leaves die down. Store the bulbs dry in any convenient spot; they need no special treatment until it is time to start a new season early the following autumn. Repot when the old container is filled with roots almost to the breaking point.

VELTHEIMIA VIRIDIFOLIA (above) BLOOMS IN EARLY SPRING IN A CONSERVATORY AT LONGWOOD GARDENS, KENNETT SQUARE, PENNSYLVANIA. THE WAVY-EDGED LEAVES IN A BASAL ROSETTE BEGIN ACTIVE GROWTH IN AUTUMN, FOLLOWING A WARM, DRY SUMMER, AND NEED A COOL BUT FROST-FREE, SUNNY PLACE IN WINTER.

CHAPTER
FIVE

TREES,
SHRUBS, AND
VINES

Whenever gardeners who love woody plants get together, the conversation invariably turns at some point to why the public is satisfied to grow so many of so few plants. While having more and more plants but less and less of a selection at the local nursery or garden center may be thought of as a sign of our times, Liberty Hyde Bailey remarked on just this sort of trend in his day, in the early years of the twentieth century. Dr. Howard Irwin, a former director of both the New York Botanical Garden in the Bronx and Clark Botanic Garden on Long Island, New York, says the practice is rooted in the general public's habit of shopping for plants only when under the influence of acute spring fever. This means when we get the urge to plant one fine day, we rush to the local garden center and buy what is beautiful and blooming right then. The result is that in a world of fascinating diversity we choose instead to plant the same things as our neighbors. In doing so we miss out on a lot. ❧ *There are other choices if we only look for them. I have nothing against forsythia, for example; in fact, hardly a winter goes by that a big bouquet of forced forsythia branches does not grace my living room. But in my garden, where there will never be enough room for everything I want to grow, there will probably not be any forsythia. Several alternatives to the ubiquitous forsythia are presented in this chapter, among them* Corylopsis, Chimonanthus, *and* Stachyurus. *I don't think this attitude makes me a plant snob, it is just being creative about what I choose to allow into my personal garden space.* ❧ *An-*

other basic pitfall with plants in this category — trees, shrubs, and vines — is that once planted and established, they seem so permanent. Try digging up a small shrub; it will likely turn out to be much more of a job than anticipated; conversely, a task that appears monumental is simply never undertaken. When we become unhappy with the woody plants in our gardens, we tend to leave them alone anyway. The result is that gardens and landscapes are often filled with too many plants of too little diversity. 🙠 In no aspect of the gardener's repertoire are there more under-grown and overlooked candidates than among the woodies. Many are native plants

WHEN TREES OF *CORNUS MAS* BLOOM (preceding pages) AT THE CONSERVATORY GARDEN IN NEW YORK CITY, URBAN DWELLERS KNOW THAT WINTER IS GIVING WAY TO SPRING. *BUDDLEIA ALTERNIFOLIA* (left), AT THE ATLANTA BOTANICAL GARDEN IN SPRING, YIELDS FRAGRANT BLOOMS.

awaiting a grower with vision who will dare to treat them with the same respect given to exotic species and named cultivars. Besides specialist growers and their catalogues, good places to look for out-of-the-ordinary trees and shrubs are in the systematic collections of botanic gardens and arboreta. Keep in mind, however, that when a plant is being grown for scientific study it may not necessarily be pruned or trained to bring out its best. A gardener who is able to look at a woody plant as raw material can see the qualities it might possess over its relatively long life.

TREES AND SHRUBS

ARONIA

The genus *Aronia*, a group of decorative, deciduous shrubs from the Rose Family native to North America, is not nearly as well known to gardeners as it should be. Plantsman Ralph Bailey was particularly enamored of *A. arbutifolia*, red chokeberry, a shrub to nine feet high which he describes as "dependable and attractive". The plant's rather oblongish leaves grow three inches long, and turn brilliant red in autumn. In mid- to late spring red chokeberry bears dense clusters of white or pink-tinged flowers. Bailey also described the bright red fruits which appear in late autumn and retain their color into winter. It is readily suited to informal plantings, and handsome in woodland settings and the wild garden.

The aronia is easily grown in almost any soil, but probably performs best where the soil is moist fairly deep, at least through the early stages of growth. Propagation is possible by seeds, cuttings, layers, or by division and removal of sucker growth. The plant is hardy to Zone 4.

BUDDLEIA

Butterfly bush or summer-lilac, *Buddleia davidii*, is usually among the first of the summer-flowering shrubs of which new gardeners become aware. Relatively few gardeners know *B. alternifolia*, which blooms in midspring and has a graceful fountain habit and pale lilac color that sets it quite apart from other plants blooming at this time. The fountain buddleia is also fragrant, especially enjoyable if sited so that the cascading branches, surrounded all along their length with blossoms, seem to reach out to greet one also may be passing by or standing in their midst. This shrub is also remarkably drought-tolerant once established and is now increasingly recognized as an appropriate plant for Xeriscaping.

Buddleia alternifolia is from China and winter hardy in Zones 5 to 9, or to about −10°F. It blooms in midspring on wood formed the previous year, so an extremely cold winter may reduce or even obliterate the current season's flowering, but new shoots will probably rise again from the roots. Give the plant a major annual pruning after flowering. For a change from its natural bushy fountain shape, this species can be trained as a stylish tree-form standard. Like many of the plants in this book, the fountain buddleia is somehow more refined, more desirable, than its more commonly grown relatives.

THIS IMPRESSIVE DISPLAY OF *CALLICARPA* FRUIT (opposite) WAS COLLECTED FROM THE BEAUTYBERRY COLLECTION AT THE BROOKLYN BOTANIC GARDEN IN EARLY NOVEMBER, BEFORE A KILLING FROST. THEY ARE SPECTACULAR IN AN AUTUMN LANDSCAPE.

CALLICARPA

Other plants besides this one have purple berries, but hardly any compare with the beauty berries, deciduous shrubs belonging to the Verbena Family and hailing from tropical and temperate regions of the Americas. Clusters of small pink, blue, or white flowers in summer are followed by many berries, bright

Flower arrangers find the flowered and berried branches irresistible, although the berries tend to part company from the branches rather soon — which is not to say that they aren't lovely in a harvest bouquet. The beautyberry drops its leaves before its berries. If there should be an early snow or ice storm

purple, purple-red, or lilac violet (white in *Callicarpa americana lactea*). Ralph Bailey, who served as garden editor for both *House Beautiful* and *House and Garden* magazines, once wrote that *C. dichotoma* ". . . is the most attractive and the hardiest species" (it is hardy to Zone 6). The shrub grows to four feet, with leaves to three inches long, their edges toothed in the upper half. The pink flowers are followed in the late summer by clusters of ornamental lilac violet berries.

while the berries are still at the peak of plumpness and color, get a camera! The stems may sometimes be winter-killed, but new growth from the base will bloom and bear fruit the same season, if the plant grows in rich soil and full sun.

Grow a tubbed callicarpa and bring it inside to a big, light, airy, cool greenhouse or sun room for an extended season. Also try contrasting red poinsettias against these berries, perhaps with some rosy and pink holiday cacti.

CALYCANTHUS

The calycanthus are of chief interest for their aromatic leaves and spicy flowers in spring. Gardeners who are impressed by obvious showiness from brightly colored blossoms may overlook these plants; their subtle flowers are reddish brown and likely to be hidden beneath the foliage canopy. Carolina allspice, *Calycanthus floridus*, is hardiest (to Zone 4) and the most fragrant. Pale sweetshrub, *C. fertilis*, is similar. Both can grow four to eight feet tall. *Calycanthus occidentalis* has a more open form; it grows to 12 feet, and in California (its native state), is protected on the preservation list; so it is not to be picked or dug up from the wild. All calycanthus originate in North America, and their glossy but coarse leaves turn yellow in autumn. They do best in rich, well-drained soil, in sun or shade.

CAMELLIA

Until recently the official party line on the camellia in North America has been that it was a glorious flowering shrub for mild climates only, or for glass-enclosed winter gardens in the North. But there are changes in the camellia world. New varieties are increasingly cold-hardy, fragrant, and available in yellow as well as the usual white and pink. A sasanqua cultivar, 'Shishi Gashira', blooms in late December outdoors in the Brooklyn Botanic Garden, in Zone 7; its semidouble flowers are slightly fragrant, with yellow centers surrounded by rosy pink petals touched with white. Hybrids involving *Camellia saluensis* are a source of greater cold-hardiness; also consider the species *C. maliflora*, *C. oleifera*, *C. vernalis*, and cultivars of *C. × williamsii* for colder climates. The camellia is a member of the Tea Family. The tea of commerce comes from the leaf buds of *C. sinensis*.

CALYCANTHUS FLORIDUS (above) IS THE HARDIEST AND MOST FRAGRANT OF THE SWEET SHRUBS. *CAMELLIA SASANQUA × OLEIFERA* (below) BLOOMS OCTOBER TO NOVEMBER AT BROOKLYN BOTANIC GARDEN. *CHIMONANTHUS PRAECOX*, BLOOMS AT THE EARLIEST DATE IT CAN MUSTER.

CHIMONANTHUS

Chimonanthus (not to be confused with fringe tree, *Chionanthus*) is a genus of two shrubs from Asia, *C. praecox* or wintersweet being the one most often cultivated. It thrives in a sandy loam, preferably with leaf mold added, and can be propagated from seeds or cuttings. Some catalogues list this plant as *Meratia fragrans*, which gives a clue to the fragrance of the yellow flowers that bloom in late winter (the specific epithet *praecox* tells us "very early"). Wintersweet is a deciduous shrub from China that can grow to 10 feet high and as wide. The lustrous opposite green leaves appear later than the flowers, and grow to six inches long. Wintersweet is effective in a mixed shrubbery border, or at the back of a flower bed, and especially trained on a wall in an espalier pattern. In mild climates this shrub blooms all winter; farther north to Zone 7, the buds are nudged into fully open, deliciously scented blooms by the merest hint of a winter thaw. A specimen espaliered against a south-facing wall may bloom earlier and longer, and with such protection might survive most winters in climates colder than Zone 7.

CHIONANTHUS

Chionanthus (not to be confused with *Chimonanthus*) is the fringe tree. More specifically, *C. virginicus* is known as old-man's-beard or Grandaddy Graybeard, which, depending on your imagination, may or may not sound like something you'd like sprouting in your garden. Fringe tree grows wild from Pennsylvania to Florida, westward to Texas, and gets on in climates having quite cold winters, to Zone 5. It grows up to

The fringe trees need sun and do best in an open, bright location. They prosper in deep, rich loam enhanced with compost or well-rotted manure. Plant or transplant in spring or autumn. Propagate by cuttings or seeds sown in a cool place in early spring. Cuttings of two- to three-inch-long semiripe shoots will root if inserted in a propagation frame in early summer. Chinese fringe tree has leaves and flowers that are

30 feet tall, with wonderfully scented, feathery snow-white blossoms that flutter in the gentlest of breezes, creating a shimmery effect that is magical. Another species cultivated, *C. retusus*, is from China and Korea, hardy only to Zone 6, and also bears many white flowers in terminal panicles in early summer.

smaller than those of the native species, but the plant itself also is smaller, growing to only 18 feet, and therefore is probably a better choice for more intimate garden settings. Chionanthus leaves turn bright golden yellow in autumn, and established female trees bear bunches of dark blue, grape-like fruits that delight birds.

FRINGE TREE UP CLOSE (left) AND A SPECIMEN AT
BROOKLYN BOTANIC GARDEN (right) SHOW
THE FEATHERY, SCENTED BLOSSOMS.

CORNUS MAS

CORYLOPSIS

Cornelian cherry, *Cornus mas*, represents one distinct facet of a genus that gives us some of the temperate climate's favorite flowering trees and shrubs; and even one ground cover — the bunchberry, *C. canadensis*, a neat, attractive evergreen subshrub to six inches high with a creeping rootstock. Cornelian cherry is a large, vigorous, spreading tree growing to 25 feet, with lustrous green, oval leaves to four inches long. It is hardy to Zone 4 and seems to thrive in city air; there are especially impressive specimens on either side of the entry steps into the Conservatory Garden in New York City's Central Park. They are among this landscape's earliest blossoms, and the trees themselves manage to thrive despite their close proximity to pollution-belching buses and automobiles that blast them day

BUTTERCUP WINTER HAZEL, *CORYLOPSIS PAUCIFLORA*, IS GIVEN A PROMINENT POSITION NEAR THE GATES TO THE ROCK GARDEN AT NEW YORK BOTANICAL GARDEN (right).

and night all the year long. (They are also somewhat shaded by extremely tall, old primary shade trees.) Cornelian cherry is an understory tree, adaptable to any garden situation where there may be somewhat less than abundant direct sun.

A special appeal of the Cornelian cherry to the adventurous gardener is that its tiny clusters of yellow flowers appear in early spring before the leaves, and are followed in late summer by scarlet fruit that is acidic but edible. The variety 'Flava' has yellow fruit and in 'Aureoelegantissima' the leaves are variegated creamy white, and blushed rosy red. The branches of *C. mas* are readily forced into early bloom indoors; it is a shame that more gardeners do not know and grow this shrubby tree, for it is a real garden trooper.

Fragrant winter hazel, *Corylopsis*, is a deciduous shrub from Asia, with alternate leaves and yellow flowers in short, nodding clusters at the dawn of spring, before the ribbed leaves unfurl and before the ubiquitous forsythia begin to stir. It belongs to the Witch Hazel Family and thrives in light, peaty soil. Perhaps best known among the gardening cognoscenti is *C. pauciflora*, the buttercup winter hazel, a low to medium shrub

which grows four to six feet tall and as wide, with ovate leaves to three inches long that are pale beneath. The new growth has a red hue that is most attractive. The pale yellow flowers appear in clusters of two or three. It is hardy from Zones 5 to 8, but a protected place is required if it is planted in Zone 5. This species is more tolerant of alkaline soil than others in the genus. It will adapt well in light shade with a moisture-retentive, well-drained soil into which a generous amount of organic matter has been worked. Prune after spring bloom, or cut branches for forcing early indoors.

COTINUS

The genus *Cotinus* belongs to the Cashew Family and is best known to gardeners for the smoketree, *C. coggygria*. A smoketree is a spreading Eurasian shrub growing to 15 feet tall, with rounded leaves to three inches long, narrowed at the base. In late summer appears a profusion of feathery, pinkish fruiting clusters to 10 inches long; they look like clouds of smoke hovering around the bush. In autumn the leaves turn yellow and purple. In the variety 'Purpureus' the leaves and fruiting panicles are dark purplish. This cultivar is hardy to Zone 5 or 6, and there is a specimen at the University of Minnesota School of Horticulture, in St. Paul. The cultivar 'Royal Purple' grows

SMOKETREE'S FEATHERY PINK FRUITING CLUSTERS (opposite) INSPIRE THE POPULAR NAME FOR *COTINUS COGGYGRIA*. TRUE QUINCE (right) CAN BE SEEN AT BROOKLYN BOTANIC GARDEN.

to 10 feet and has red leaves that change to purple; it is the best choice for a limited space. *C. obovatus* is an erect native American shrub or tree to 25 feet high, with rounded leaves to five inches and small, yellowish flowers in early summer.

Depending on how cotinus is trained and pruned it can become a large shrub or a small tree. It is outstanding as part of a flowering shrubbery border, or as background for almost any kind of flower garden. If trained as a small tree the cotinus can be a most unusual accent plant in the landscape, as a single specimen, or planted allée-style along a garden walk or pathway. Smoketree grows easily in any ordinary, well-drained soil that is not too rich. Once established, the roots are also surprisingly resourceful in times of drought.

CYDONIA

Cydonia is a member of the Rose Family that will grow wherever apples and pears succeed. A native of Persia, it was known to the Romans as the "apple from Cydon". *Cydonia oblonga*, the edible quince, is a small, much-branched tree that needs deeply spaded, fairly heavy soil that is moist but also well drained. The pear-shaped fruit turns golden in autumn and is useful, when cooked, for delicious jams and jellies, alone or combined with other fruits. A low basket or bowl of ripe quince placed

in a room will scent the air delightfully. The cultivar 'Orange' is also recommended for pies and juice. 'Pineapple' was named by Luther Burbank for the flavor it imparts to jelly. 'Smyrna' has the advantages of storing longer than any other quince and having a strong fragrance. 'Van Damen', developed by Burbank in 1891, is the progeny of a cross between 'Orange' and 'Portugal', a heavy producer of spice-flavored fruits. Any of these cultivars will make a most ornamental tree, cold hardy to Zone 4, and slow growing, 10 to 25 feet tall. The quince is ideal as part of a flower border or herb garden.

DAPHNE

Daphne represents a genus of small evergreen and deciduous shrubs from Europe and Asia that is universally admired yet not readily available. All daphnes grow best in a well-drained, sandy loam with leaf mold, and in part sun to partial shade. They are long-lived shrubs of tidy habit that need no pruning. Transplanting is difficult, so attempt moving only young stock. Garland-flower, *D. cneorum*, is a dense evergreen about knee-high, with short clusters of bright rose-pink flowers in spring, and often again in late summer; it is hardy to Zone 6, 5 if protected. *Daphne genkwa* is deciduous, to three feet, with slender, arching branches that display the lightly fragrant, luminous, lilac-colored flowers appearing in early spring, before the leaves; hardy to Zone 7. Winter daphne, *D. odora*, is evergreen, to four feet, with extremely fragrant rose-purple or whitish flowers in dense heads in March and April. This species is a favorite for spring flower shows and often cultivated in a large pot in a cool greenhouse where the fragrance can be easily appreciated. The variety 'Aureo-Marginata' is the most fragrant, hardier than *D. odora*, with dark crimson buds opening to clustered white flowers in early spring. The large glossy leaves are lightly margined with cream on a shrub that slowly reaches to five feet. It grows best in a cool, moist location where there is light shade in summer and is hardy only in Zones 8 to 10. *Daphne caucasica*, a deciduous shrub which grows to about five feet, has terminal heads of fragrant white flowers in late spring. Once established, this species from the Caucasus is more drought-tolerant than the other daphnes.

A current favorite is *D.* × *burkwoodii*, 'Carol Mackie', which offers gold-banded foliage, a compact habit all year, and the bonus in late spring to early summer of tremendous numbers of pale pink, richly fragrant flowers. It is rated for hardiness in Zones 4 to 8.

ENKIANTHUS

Enkianthus campanulatus is a distinctive deciduous shrub from Japan, hardy to Zone 5, that is inexplicably neglected by today's gardeners. It belongs to the Heath Family, so the need for slightly acid soil, with lots of sphagnum peat moss mixed in, comes as no surprise. Best growth also occurs in soil that is moist and well-drained. Whorled branches have alternate leaves, crowded toward the end of the branchlets, on a shrub that can grow to almost any desired size, from 10 to 25 feet high. The bell-shaped flowers, creamy to yellow or even orangish with red veins, to a half-inch long, appear in great profusion in mid-spring. There are also red- and white-flowered cultivars. In autumn the leaves turn a brilliant scarlet. Another species of particular note is *E. perulatus*, a decorative, small shrub to six feet tall. The leaves, to two inches long, turn a glowing yellow and scarlet in the fall. Bell-shaped, white flowers appear in early mid-spring, before the leaves.

The best site for enkianthus offers some direct sun in the morning or afternoon, with high, open shade at midday. Little pruning is needed except for touch up removal of dead, broken, or winter-damaged growth. Because of its natural form enkianthus adapts well to espalier treatment, as an informal fan against a wall or fence that would otherwise be bare. Be sure to allow five or six inches of air space between the espalier and the wall; otherwise sunburn may occur, even in winter. In colder regions, select a site facing south or west.

PENNSYLVANIA GARDENER SALLY REATH TRAINS
ENKIANTHUS CAMPANULATUS AS AN ESPALIER
ALONG A WEST-FACING, PARTIALLY SHADED, TALL
WOOD FENCE. *LIRIOPE MUSCARI* 'VARIEGATA'' IS
THE GROUND COVER EDGING.

EXOCHORDA

Pearl-bush, *Exochorda*, named for its pearly buds, has always been something of a connoisseur's plant, popular among those in the know, but unknown to the masses and not often seen at local nurseries. A cultivar out of *Exochorda* × *macrantha* called 'The Bride' is perhaps the finest, a tidy, dense shrub of gracefully arching branches to five or six feet tall and as wide. The branches are completely covered with large, white flowers in late spring to early summer, and hardly any flowering shrub could be more beautiful or more welcome at this stage of the gardening year. While visiting the gardens at Great Dixter in England in late May, I was impressed that 'The Bride' was given a prominent place among the world's treasured plants.

A MEMBER OF THE WITCH HAZEL FAMILY THAT GROWS WILD IN GEORGIA, *FOTHERGILLA MAJOR* (upper) IS LOVELY IN SPRING BLOOM, BUT THE REAL SHOW COMES IN AUTUMN WHEN THE LEAVES TURN YELLOW AND RED.

Exochorda belongs to the Rose Family and is cold hardy to well below 0°F. Site it in a sunny location where the soil is humusy and well-drained. Prune annually, following bloom. Remove from the base the branches that have flowered most heavily, in order to make way for new shoots that will give the next year's blooms. Regular pruning maintains exochorda's airy openness. Exochorda species are readily propagated from seeds, best sown under glass as soon as they are ripe; 'The Bride' and other cultivars can be increased by layers or softwood cuttings in spring or summer. Companion plants for exochordas include ground covers such as vinca, pachysandra, and English ivy, and flowers such as pansy, viola, lunaria, sweet William, and cottage and other late tulips. More unusual partners include grasses such as dwarf blue fescue.

FOTHERGILLA

The fothergillas belong to the Witch Hazel Family and are native to the southeastern United States. In the early spring *Fothergilla gardenii* (which is also called witch alder) bears creamy white, honey-scented blooms in delicate, airy, inch-long spikes. They are followed by leathery, dark green foliage that turns into a spectacular display of glowing yellow and orange-red as the cooler weather and longer nights of autumn arrive. This extravaganza of color is best achieved in full sun. *Fothergilla gardenii*, which grows only two to three feet tall and is hardy in Zones 5 to 8, makes an ideal bedmate with smaller azaleas and other rhododendrons. Despite its charm in spring and cooling green in summer, it is for its autumn foliage color that fothergilla is cherished. Give it a moisture-retentive, acid soil and take care that the site will remain moist all summer; drying out is a major problem for fothergilla in hot weather. It will grow in sun or shade, however, and was at one time ranked among the top shrubs cultivated in American gardens. Now the fothergilla is difficult to obtain, but it is invaluable for small spaces and wet situations. *Fothergilla* 'Blue Mist' is a recent introduction discovered at the Morris Arboretum of the University of Pennsylvania in Philadelphia. It is a three- to four-foot deciduous shrub that blooms in the spring in the manner of *gardenii*, but then becomes clothed in frosty blue foliage that gradually darkens until in autumn it turns splendidly yellow and red. This is an ideal shrub to combine with other woodland and shade-loving plants, or to use as a focal point in a small garden. A shady location brings out the blue in the leaves. *Fothergilla major*, from Georgia, grows to 10 feet and bears flowers and leaves together.

Propagate fothergillas from seeds, or by layers (allow two years), *F. gardenii* from suckers and root cuttings.

HYDRANGEA

As often seems the case, the more desirable species and varieties of *Hydrangea* are not necessarily the ones most often cultivated. The best known is the bigleaf hydrangea or florist's hortensia, *H. macrophylla*, the ubiquitous Easter and Mother's Day potted plant, with large heads of flowers, usually very blue or very pink, occasionally white. But in the connoisseur's garden one is more likely to find other hydrangeas. There is the climbing hydrangea, *H. anomala petiolaris*, a root climber growing to 50 feet on a wall with fragrant white flowers in early summer. The flowers appear in loose clusters to a foot wide, with white, sterile blossoms around the edges.

Oak-leaved hydrangea, *H. quercifolia*, is one of the finest ornamentals ever introduced, particularly the cultivar 'Snow Queen', selected by nurseryman William Flemer III from a stand of seedlings. 'Snow Queen' reaches five to seven feet with a similar spread in a few years and will mature at around 10 feet. Both the species and cultivar thrive in deep shade as well as full sun, but the cultivar requires more water in times of drought. Also choice are the lacecaps, such as *H. macrophylla* 'Serrata', with flat, mid- to late-summer flower heads that are pink, lilac, or white in the inner part, blue or pink in the outer flowers. Hardly any shrub matches lacecap hydrangea for the intricate beauty and color coordination of its blooms. The common peegee hydrangea, *H. paniculata* 'Grandiflora', can be pruned into a stylish small tree, to 20 feet high. Most hydrangeas are hardy to Zone 5 or 6; the peegee to Zone 4.

THE LACECAP *HYDRANGEA SERRATA* (opposite, lower) IS AMONG THE PLANTS TO WHICH THE BALLARDS OF PHILADELPHIA HAVE CHOSEN TO GIVE SPACE AND AFFECTION.

ILEX

The right holly in the right place is one of the garden's best all-around plants. There are thought to be a thousand different hollies, ranging from one-foot shrubs to 80-foot trees. Hollies are dioecious; plants with male (staminate) flowers and plants with female (pistillate) flowers must both be present in order for berries to develop on the female plants. *Ilex cornuta* and *I. laevigata*, however, appear to bear fruit without the usual

cross-pollination. English holly, *I. aquifolium*, is hardy to Zone 6 but cannot tolerate hot, dry summers. Chinese holly, *I. cornuta*, hardy to Zone 7, is favored in the South. Japanese holly, *I. crenata*, grows to Zone 6; some varieties resemble boxwood and are used where *Buxus* could not thrive. American holly, *I. opaca*, is hardy to Zone 5. Yaupon, *I. vomitoria*, is an evergreen native to the southeastern United States, hardy to Zone 7; it grows to 25 feet and can be sheared as a hedge. One more species not to be missed is winterberry, *I. verticillata*, leafless in winter so the berries really show off.

ITEA

Considering the elegant beauty and fragrant blossoms of *Itea virginica*, it is no wonder that the sweetspire, or Virginia-willow, would be a favorite of plantsmen Ralph Bailey and Thomas Henry Dodd, Jr. Sweetspire is a deciduous shrub to eight feet tall, with slender, erect branches. Finely toothed leaves to three inches long turn a brilliant red in autumn. These qualities, along with the midspring show of white flowers in upright clusters of up to six inches, make sweetspire more garden-worthy than many plants far more common.

Sweetspire is native from New Jersey, Zone 6, southward to Florida and Louisiana. Bailey noted that the plant was not par-ticular about soil as long as it was not too dry, and would grow in either sun or shade. He also observed that sweetspire would grow in soil that was "quite moist," suggesting that itea would grow well in a partly sunny woodland garden in a low-lying area inclined to protracted (but not boggy) wetness. *Itea ilicifolia*, the holly-leaf itea, is an evergreen to 10 feet tall, hardy to Zone 7, with spiny leaves that resemble holly, to four inches long. The greenish white flowers are arranged in drooping clusters to 12 inches long and are especially effective next to a path where they can be seen at close range. *Itea yunnanensis* is another evergreen shrub, to six feet, with four-inch leaves and six-inch-long clusters of white flowers.

All of the iteas are popular with flower arrangers; so that one may wish to grow them in mixed shrubbery borders where stems cut for arranging won't be missed as they might in a formal garden. Propagate new plants by division of the roots in spring, from softwood cuttings in summer, or by sow-ing the seeds. *Hortus Third*, published in 1976, places Itea in the Saxifrage Family. *The American Horticultural Society Encyclopedia of Garden Plants* (1989) places Itea in the Grossularia Family, along with *Ribes* (the genus of currant and gooseberry).

KIRENGESHOMA

When they first meet *Kirengeshoma palmata*, knowledgeable gar-deners often think it is a new plant. But it has been in cultiva-tion in North America, far from its native wooded mountains of southern Japan, for more than a century. As a member of the Saxifrage Family, it is in royal company — the family con-tains many cherished ornamental plants. Yet kirengeshoma it-self remains mysteriously obscure. It is technically a perennial

herb, but I have placed it in this chapter because from mid-summer to frost it looks like a shrub with the mass of a ro-bust, large-leaved hydrangea, *H. macrophylla*, to a range between four and five-and-a-half feet tall and as wide. The plant's maple-like, palmately lobed leaves grow to eight inches long. Toward the tips of the stems are an endless supply of rounded buds that become showy yellow flowers, to an inch and a half long, waxy but also suggesting those of flowering maple, *Abutilon*. Kirengeshoma thrives in humusy, well-drained but generously moistened soil, in half sun to half shade.

LINDERA

Spicebush, *Lindera benzoin*, is an easily grown shrub belonging to the Laurel Family. Unlike many of its relatives, it is hardy to Zone 6 and native to North America; most species in the genus are tropical Asians. Also listed as *Benjoin aestivale*, spicebush is a deciduous shrub to 15 feet tall and a familiar inhabitant of woods from Maine to Florida and westward to Texas. Its leaves, to five inches long, turn a clear golden yellow in autumn and are especially effective as a background for chrysanthemums and hardy asters. The dense clusters of tiny, greenish yellow flowers make an attractive display in very early spring, before the leaves unfold. Butterflies are attracted to the spicebush, and the leaves, when crushed, emit a pungent fragrance derived from its oil, which once had wide medicinal use as tincture of benzoin. The female plants produce scarlet, oblong, spicy berries that are colorful long after the leaves have dropped.

In the garden, spicebush is treated as a large shrub or small understory tree; it can also be espaliered as an informal fan. The plant thrives in moist soil and tolerates some shade. It will also grow in full sun but will require more irrigation in dry weather, or at least a three-inch mulch to preserve soil moisture. Lindera is best transplanted when small, and then only in early spring. *Lindera benzoin* is on the preservation list in Kentucky, which means in that state it is illegal to pick or dig up a wild spicebush. Propagate new plants from seeds sown as soon as they are ripe, or by softwood cuttings in summer. A similar plant, *L. obtusiloba*, from mountainous regions of China, Korea, and Japan, is a deciduous shrub or tree to 30 feet high; its three-lobed, five-inch leaves follow the yellow flowers.

MAGNOLIA

The genus *Magnolia* contains evergreen and deciduous trees and shrubs, found from the Himalayas to Japan, and eastern North America to Central America and Venezuela. Magnolias are treasured for their handsome foliage, breathtaking flowers and, sometimes, their fragrance. *Magnolia ashei*, native from western Florida to Texas, is one of the lesser known, more desirable species that is garden-worthy, brought to my attention by plantsman Thomas Henry Dodd, Jr. of Alabama. *Magnolia ashei* is similar to the more common *M. macrophylla* (the large-leaved cucumber tree, which grows to 50 feet), but is smaller and more readily accommodated in limited space. The creamy white flowers, four to six inches wide, have an exquisite profile as the buds begin to open. Gardeners familiar only with the white southern magnolia, *M. grandiflora*, and the dusty pinks of the early spring Japanese species may be surprised to learn that there are also yellow magnolias. *Magnolia acuminata cordata* 'Miss Honeybee', a selection of the native American yellow cucumber tree, bears bright yellow flowers in late spring to early summer, and sometimes again later in the same season; it is suitable for Zones 4 to 9. 'Elizabeth' has fragrant, rich, clear yellow flowers that appear before the leaves; it was developed by breeder Evamarie Sperber in a program sponsored by the Brooklyn Botanic Garden and has survived temperatures to −20°F.

In general, magnolias need a location in sun to half shade with humusy, loam-based soil that is well drained but deeply moist. Propagate by sowing seeds outdoors in autumn (or stratify them indoors before planting), from cuttings rooted under glass, or by layers put down in the spring. Magnolias resent disturbance; transplant only before new growth starts.

LINDERA BENZOIN OFFERS INTEREST IN EVERY SEASON. AUTUMN LEAF COLOR IS SUPERB, AS CAPTURED HERE IN EARLY DECEMBER AT BROOKLYN BOTANIC GARDEN.

THE NAME OF *MAGNOLIA VESEYI* (left) SUGGESTS A
GOBLET OR CHALICE PROFILE. *MAGNOLIA*
'ELIZABETH' (above) IS SUPERB YELLOW FOR
MIDSPRING. *MAGNOLIA ASHEI* (opposite) IS A
SMALL, CHOICE TREE.

OCHNA

Bird's-eye bush, *Ochna*, describes upwards of a hundred species of tropical trees and shrubs from the Old World. They are not uncommon to gardens in the tropics, but only one is much cultivated in North America: *O. serrulata* (which is sometimes sold under the name of *O. multiflora*, another recognized species that is not thought to be in cultivation). This species, seen outdoors mostly in southern California (Zone 10), is originally from South Africa. It is a somewhat irregular shrub which grows to five feet tall and has alternate, toothed, leathery leaves and primrose yellow, fragrant flowers in spring. These are succeeded by the calyx that turns from green to red and green berries that turn black as they ripen. The berries are rather reminiscent of "Mouseketeer" ears, and are responsible for the unofficial popular name: Mickey-Mouse plant. Where the weather is too cold for ochna it makes an ideal indoor-outdoor container specimen. The potted plant can be allowed to develop normally or can be dwarfed and trained as a bonsai to enhance its artistic merit. Ochna thrives in a loam-based soil or potting mix that includes some sand and generous amounts of organic matter such as sphagnum peat moss and well-rotted leaf mold. Propagate by sowing fresh seeds about one-half inch deep or by taking cuttings of half-ripened wood in late summer. Ochna does best in full sun and in a place, indoors or out, where there is unhampered movement of fresh air. As a potted plant, keep it cool but frost-free and on the dry side from late autumn until early spring.

PONCIRUS TRIFOLIATA PRODUCES A LAVISH DISPLAY OF FRAGRANT BLOSSOMS IN SPRING AND TWO-INCH FURRY, INEDIBLE FRUITS IN EARLY AUTUMN (near right). J. LIDDON PENNOCK, JR., TRAINED HIS INTO TREE-FORM STANDARDS (far right).

PONCIRUS

The hardy orange, *Poncirus trifoliata*, stands alone in this genus from China, a deciduous, very thorny shrub or small tree, to 25 feet. It is the hardiest of the citrus, definitely surviving in

Zone 6 (Zone 5 if protected), and it is used commercially as the rootstock onto which various of the family's more tender fruits are grafted. In early spring, before the leaves appear, the branches become garlands of white, bedecked with intensely fragrant blossoms. The dark green, leathery leaflets come next and the developing fruits are all but forgotten until one day in early autumn they seem suddenly hung everywhere among the branches, as if the tree were decorated in preparation for a harvest party. The yellow fruit, to two inches across, is very softly furry, orange-like, full of seeds, and too acidic to be edible. Several tossed into a bowl of potpourri, however, will give the house a haunting, spicy fragrance for several weeks.

ROSA POLYANTHA

I suppose it could be considered obsessive to collect only moss roses or only roses having striped petals, but what about that small grouping known as the Easter roses? These early polyanthas came from the Danish breeder Poulsen, and their nickname derives from the tradition of selling the bushes potted and in bloom for the Easter holiday. I became acquainted with them as tree-form standards 24 inches tall, which gardening columnist C. Z. Guest grows all year in 12-inch pots. They spend summers outdoors, winters in a cool greenhouse

or sun pit, and Easter in the house proper where they can be admired at close range.

My favorite Easter rose is a color that reminds me of orange sherbet only more so, but without being too orange. The rounded blossoms are borne in great clusters, their abundance and beauty offering a glimpse into what the Empress Josephine saw at Malmaison in the precursors of the roses Poulsen developed a hundred or so gardening seasons later. Although smaller in size, the inward rounding of these roses reminds me of the Bourbons. Last April I saw Easter roses in a private garden in Natchez, Mississippi; they were a darker orange shade, almost orange-red, and seemed to glow from within.

STACHYURUS PRAECOX

In the year I worked at the Brooklyn Botanic Garden and walked through the grounds nearly every day, the *Stachyurus praecox* in bloom in late March stands out in my memory as the single most unusual sight I encountered. Some plants probably succeed by being at their best when hardly anything else is, but that is certainly not true of this one. *Stachyurus praecox* would stand out in any crowd, at any time of year, even a midwinter thaw. But as luck would have it, stachyurus blooms somewhere between late February and April, provided it

doesn't get killed by frost. The handsome deciduous shrub grows to 10 feet, with slender, spreading branches and oval to lance-shaped leaves to five inches long. The small, yellow, bell-shaped flowers are borne in drooping clusters three to five inches long, which hang down from all the branches. Stachyurus is beautiful at a distance, from which the plant's perfect form can be appreciated. Stachyurus thrives in sandy loam with plenty of leaf mold worked in at planting time and thereafter applied annually as a top-dressing or mulch. Stachyurus is rated cold-hardy to Zone 7, Zone 6 if protected. Propagate by seeds, cuttings, or layers.

STEWARTIA

Besides being difficult to transplant, the sin of *Stewartia* may be that it is too beautiful; otherwise how can such an extraordinary plant's failure to gain widespread acceptance be explained? *Stewartia ovata* is a deciduous shrub or tree, to 15 feet tall or more, with five-inch-long oval leaves that turn orange and scarlet in autumn. The waxy, saucer-like white flowers to three inches across have orange anthers and appear in spring. In variety *grandiflora* the slightly larger flowers are set off with attractive purple stamens; if a member of the vegetable kingdom can have "Elizabeth Taylor eyes," these blossoms do.

From any perspective the stewartias rate among the most

POULSEN EASTER ROSES (far left) BLOOM IN APRIL IN A NATCHEZ GARDEN. "VERY EARLY AND UNIQUE" DESCRIBES THE FLOWERS OF *STACHYRUS PRAECOX* (near left). *STEWARTIA OVATA* 'GRANDIFLORA' (right) IS A SPRING BLOOMER.

beautiful of native American shrubs. They are usually found on mountain slopes of the southeastern United States. Stewartias are hardy to Zone 6 and are well suited to use as specimen trees in a lawn or as accents in shrubbery borders. Propagate new plants from seeds (that have first stratifed for several months), softwood cuttings, or layers. Stewartias grow best in rich, moist, peaty loam in partial shade. Never purchase one unless it is established in a container, from which transplanting will be possible without root disturbance. *Stewartia malachodendron* grows to 12 feet, with noteworthy bark and four-inch, blue-anthered, white flowers in summer. *Stewartia pseudocamellia* is a Japanese tree growing to 30 feet, hardy to Zone 7, with reddish, flaky bark, bright green three-inch leaves that turn purple in autumn, and two-and-a-half-inch, orange-anthered white flowers in summer.

TAMARIX

Members of this genus of deciduous shrubs or trees from Europe and Asia have small, alternate, scalelike leaves and a great exuberance of small, pretty flowers in clusters that give the outer third of a blooming plant the appearance of pink, feathery fireworks going off. Tamarisks thrive near the sea and are useful as sand-binders. They tolerate both dry and humid climates, either windy or calm. How is it that such a beautiful, adaptable plant is not taken for granted, so widely grown as to be boring? Amazingly, it has yet to be discovered by gardeners.

Plantsman Ralph Bailey rated both Athel tamarisk or salt tree, *T. aphylla,* hardy only to Zone 9 and *T. pentandra* (hardy to Zone 5) as being worthy of greater use in home and public landscapes. I have seen tamarisk grown as a silt-drifted, dry-soil windbreak in the Oklahoma Panhandle; stretching over a tall iron fence near the Sorbonne in Paris; and around a newly installed water garden and multilevel, walk-through landscape at Kew Gardens in London. Tamarisk also grows in the systematic collection at the Brooklyn Botanic Garden.

TAMARIX PENTANDRA IS PROMINENT IN A STROLL-
THROUGH WATER AND LAND GARDEN AT KEW,
THE ROYAL BOTANICAL GARDEN, IN LONDON.

VITEX

The genus *Vitex* in the Verbena Family includes deciduous and evergreen shrubs or trees that are widely disbursed about the warm and temperate regions of the world. Some gardeners consider them a bit coarse for prim shrubbery borders while others, the more adventurous and visionary garden makers, see the benefits of having Vitex, especially *V. agnus-castus*, the chaste-tree. This enthusiastic grower has the charming habit of producing small, fragrant lilac or lavender flowers, to seven inches long, in late summer; a white variety, 'Alba', is also available. At Meadowbrook Farms in Pennsylvania, vitex appear in the demonstration gardens leading from the parking lot to the garden center proper. On a midsummer visit they were courting as many butterflies as the buddleias nearby. Both are shrubs to 10 feet tall, hardy to Zone 6 or 7; although they may die to the ground in a tough winter, they will almost always return strongly from the roots. Vitex is also a proven performer in container gardens, at ground level as well as in high-rise terrace and rooftop situations with strong winds.

VITEX FLOWERS, OFTEN BLUE, CAN ALSO BE
WHITE AS IN 'ALBA'; THEY ARE FRAGRANT AND
APPEAR IN LATE SUMMER.

VINES

MALE VINES OF HARDY *ACTINIDIA KOLOMIKTA*
(above) HAVE WHITE AND PINK LEAF TIPS THAT
ARE MOST PROMINENT EARLY IN THE GROWING
SEASON. THIS IS A SPECIAL BEAUTY ON A TRELLIS
OR ARBOR, OR ESPALIERED ON A SUNNY GARDEN
WALL. BOTANIST PETER NELSON (near right)
EXPLAINS THE HEART-SHAPED LEAF OF
ARISTOLOCHIA MACROPHYLA OR *A. DURIOR.*

ACTINIDIA

The white- and pink-tipped new leaves of the male *Actinidia kolomikta* have made it one of the most prominent of the lesser known, hardy perennial vines. It is absolutely cold hardy to Zone 4. The female kolomikta vine bears plain green leaves as well as flowers and fruit, the latter apparently significant only to the plant itself. Plants of either sex — or, better yet, both entwined — make interesting container specimens for a medium- to large-size home greenhouse or sun porch. Another relatively hardy actinidia, the kiwi berry, *A. chinensis*, hardy to Zone 7, produces an edible, gooseberry-like fruit that is recommended for making preserves. It is considered of greater ornamental value than *A. arguta*, hardy to Zone 4, the female vines of which produce sweet, yellow-green fruit that is smooth-skinned (not fuzzy as in the commercial kiwi).

ARISTOLOCHIA

Dutchman's-pipe vine, known traditionally as *Aristolochia durior* but more correctly — according to recent botanical studies — as *A. macrophylla* (the name means "large-leaved"), is potentially one of the landscape highlights of late summer and autumn. The Dutchman's-pipe, with its forthrightly romantic heart-shaped leaves, has been a good choice for covering a summer porch on many a Victorian house, old and new, then and now. Another way to support the vines and turn them into an arresting shape and form in the garden is to provide a wood or bamboo cane tepee approximately eight feet tall and at least four or five feet in diameter at the base. By midsummer the luxuriant vines will be advancing well toward the summit. Hardy to Zone 4, this vigorous native species makes a dense green wall in just 60 days.

BASELLA

Malabar spinach is another name for the twining vine botanists have named *Basella alba*, a warm-weather, fast-growing substitute for spinach that also makes an ornamental vine. Even showier is the cultivar 'Rubra', with stems, petioles, and flowers

that are reddish. Train basella to a fence or on a sizable tepee. Allow plenty of space, especially in the South — this plant can become massive in a matter of weeks in hot summer weather. Space basella plants three to five feet apart, or use them individually where space allows and a vine is needed. Basella can also make a beautiful container-grown vine for outdoors, able to withstand intensely hot conditions on a terrace or rooftop. Just be sure to plant in humusy, well-drained soil and be prepared to water generously in the absence of rain.

In the North, give basella seeds a jump on the season by starting them indoors approximately eight weeks before the arrival of warm, settled weather outdoors. Keep sowings constantly warm (72°F.) and evenly moist. Start harvesting in nine to 10 weeks after planting, using the young tips as one would spinach. Basella is thought to have originated in Africa and Southeast Asia, but now has pantropical distribution.

THE RED-STEMMED MALABAR SPINACH, *BASELLA ALBA* 'RUBRA', IS A TWINING VINE THAT GROWS BY LEAPS AND BOUNDS IN HOT WEATHER. TRAIN IT ON A FENCE, TEPEE, ARBOR, OR ANY STRONG TRELLIS. HARVEST AND EAT THE TENDER TIP GROWTH THE SAME AS IF IT WERE TRUE SPINACH, RAW IN SALADS OR STEAMED AS A VEGETABLE DISH.

DOLICHOS

Purple hyacinth-bean, *Dolichos lablab*, known also as *Lablab pur-pureus*, is for all practical purposes a purple-flowering counter-part to 'Scarlet Runner' bean (see *Phaseolus*). Both vines are also available in varieties having white flowers. Purple hyacinth-bean produces large, glowing red-purple seedpods at the end of summer or in early autumn, which thrust outward from the vines in an obviously showy way. It also boasts purple stems

and leaf stalks. This fancy bean really gets growing only as the weather becomes really warm and settled, and then it races to as much as 20 feet or more by the end of summer. It is an ideal quick cover for arbors, trellises, fences, and tepees of all imaginable sizes and shapes. The vines climb by means of twining, so it does help if they have both a vertical and a hori-zontal grid of supports that are rounded (rather than squared) and not more than a half inch in diameter. Sow the seeds where they are to grow, in humusy, light loam.

PASSIFLORA

Passiflora, the genus of the passionflowers, represents a large group of perennial, mostly evergreen, tendril-climbing vines of tropical America, Asia, and Australia. They have simple or lobed, alternate leaves and, in many species, showy flowers of unusual form. The unusual structure of the flowers was once thought to be emblematic of Christ's crucifixion, giving rise to the name "passion flower". The fruit is a many-seeded berry, edible in some species and called granadilla in tropi-cal America.

Besides the fascinating species, several breeders are actively involved in assisting nature in the creation of some even more extraordinary new passifloras, including some that are quite winter-hardy. The hybrid 'Incense', for example, is root-hardy to well below 0°F. It has large, five- to seven-inch, frilly-fancy, dark purple flowers that are abundantly produced at the height of summer and into autumn, with the added bonus of a sweet-spicy fragrance. Another contemporary hybrid, from southern California breeder Patrick Worley, is 'Sunburst', with bright orange-yellow flowers (a color which is rare in this genus), and handsome, elongated foliage that is green-striped and purple on the reverse. The cultivar is hardy to 27°F. 'Coral Glow', also from Worley, is everblooming, producing coral red-pink blossoms having a long tube. It has hybrid vigor and excep-tional tolerance for warmer temperatures. 'Coral Glow' is an outstanding landscape plant for mild climates, incredibly fast-growing in summer, and the producer of many, many flowers. 'Constance Elliott', a very old cultivar out of *Passiflora caerulea*, is a most generous bloomer in pure, gleaming white.

PURPLE-LEAVED HYACINTH-BEAN, *DOLICHOS LABLAB*, MAKES AN ATTRACTIVE BACKDROP FOR A PROPER GARDEN.

PHASEOLUS

Phaseolus coccineus is the familiar, old-fashioned Scarlet runner bean that so many of us grew up with as children. Great fun for a child was — and is — to have a leafy tepee, a tripod frame covered with these fast-growing beans. Scarlet runner bean is also edible, but most of us are content with its ability to grow into a screen or canopy to 15 feet high in a matter of weeks. Although technically a perennial, it is treated mostly as an annual, an especially beautiful and effective quick cover for arbors and porches, where the large leaves and slowly brilliant red flowers make a handsome display. There is also a white-flowered cultivar, 'White Dutch Runner'. Both the red and the white forms need rich, well-drained soil and a dependable supply of water throughout the growing season, from late spring until early autumn.

RHODOCHITON

Rhodochiton volubile (a name referring to the vine's twining habit) is the purple bell vine from Mexico, suited to culture in warmer regions and usually treated as a tender annual. The vigorous leafstalks climb any handy support and will cover arbors and trellises or the roof of a greenhouse. The heart-shaped leaves have graceful, pointed tips. In summer the flowers hang from young shoots on long, threadlike stalks and have a bell-shaped red calyx and tubular, purple corolla. For indoor culture, set the plants in pots and train the shoots to stakes or allow them to trail from a hanging basket. Start seeds in late winter or early spring, in a warm window or fluorescent-light garden with bottom heat. Although this genus contains only one species, it has some well-known relatives in the Figwort Family including the snapdragon (*Antirrhinum*), *Linaria*, and pocketbook plant (*Calceolaria*).

PURPLE BELL VINE, *RHODOCHITON VOLUBILE*, IS A TENDER PERENNIAL FROM MEXICO THAT PERFORMS WELL WHEN TREATED AS AN ANNUAL. IT CAN BE SITED TO CLIMB ON A SMALL BAMBOO-CANE TEPEE OR TRELLIS, OR PLACED TO TUMBLE

FROM THE SIDES OF A HANGING BASKET OR TERRA COTTA WINDOW BOX. WHERE SUMMERS ARE TOO SHORT OR TOO COOL, RHODOCHITON CAN MAKE AN EXCEPTIONAL GREENHOUSE ROOF COVER.

CHAPTER
SIX

ORNAMENTAL
GRASSES
AND GROUND
COVERS

No aspect of the garden is being more thoroughly reconsidered now than the role of grasses and ground covers. Grasses have been a decorative element for generations. The first town dwellers planted lawn grasses and dealt with weed grasses; working and weekend farmers knew about meadow and pasture grasses. Some homeowners discovered serviceable ground covers for places that were difficult to mow, like banks and slopes. But mostly it was a sweeping expanse of manicured lawn that Americans wanted, from the building boom following World War II until sometime in the 1980s, by which time the string line trimmer had become basic equipment — for the lawn service contracted to do the work, that is. Then several changes occurred, all of which are directly shaping the way we garden in the nineties. We have come to realize that an organic approach is smart, not kooky, that maintaining the traditional lawn, which depends on a regular expenditure of a nonrenewable resource — water — is not wise. Neither is the widespread use of chemical fertilizers, pesticides, herbicides, and other materials routinely applied to those emerald swards. Low maintenance ornamental grasses and ground covers are a sensible alternative. Their utility and beauty is demonstrated in a living model, called the New American Garden, designed by landscape architects Wolfgang Oehme and James van Sweden, and installed at the U.S. National Arboretum in Washing-

ton, D.C., under the leadership of former director Dr. Henry M. Cathey. In these times of increasing environmental stresses, Dr. Cathey saw a need for "tough plants for tough times." What Dr. Cathey means is that plants are necessities to be treated with respect; and that as nearly as possible the right plant in the right place will be self-reliant — a tough plant. We are living in difficult times, environmentally and economically. But in any business the budget will cover routine maintenance of the "self-reliant" plant, so long as it fits the job description and requires minimal maintenance. Therefore, a plant that looks messy unless it is regularly deadheaded doesn't belong in the New American Garden. Instead, choose plants with other qualities — uniform growth, dependability, long blooming period, pleasing scent, maybe showy berries — and a self-cleaning habit as well. In a large public planting, the new thinking is that plants can be left in a natural state if enough are massed together in a purposeful way. Finally, in this last decade of the twentieth century, we all live under certain community pressure. Communities would be well served if the idea that shrinking the lawn, rather than committing to a larger sward, catches on. But if lawns are to shrink, something must replace them. The ornamental grasses and ground covers in this chapter offer some interesting possibilities, and the plants suggested here for ground cover are distinctly different from the usual pachysandra, ivy, and vines.

CAREX MORROWI 'VARIEGATA' (previous two pages)
IS A GRASS LOOK-ALIKE. ARDISIA JAPONICA IS A
SURPRISINGLY HARDY GROUND COVER (opposite).

ANAGALLIS

Blue pimpernel, *Anagallis monelli*, is a member of the Primrose Family from the Mediterranean. In 1980 a new form was selected by the Plant Introduction Scheme of the University of British Columbia Botanical Garden from plants grown from seed from the Alpine Garden Society of England, and given the cultivar name 'Pacific Blue'. It has since been introduced through research institution test stations in both Canada and the United States. 'Pacific Blue' is completely hardy in Vancouver (U.S.D.A. Zone 8a, Canadian Zone 8b) and should survive to at least a zone colder with some winter protection. It is a low, spreading herbaceous perennial that forms mounds eight inches tall and up to 30 inches across in a season. From late spring until hard frost in autumn, the plants are covered with gentian blue flowers.

This plant needs well-drained soil and at least six hours of direct sun a day; the flowers will not open in shade. The pink-centered, yellow-stamened, five-petaled blossoms, which can be up to an inch across, look their most radiant blue when back- or cross-lighted by the sun. Thus, 'Pacific Blue' can be especially effective as ground cover in a raised planting bed, or spilling from or over a dry wall at near eye level. Another effective use of blue pimpernel is as ground cover in a large container, such as a tub holding a tree, flowering shrub, or dwarf conifer. 'Pacific Blue' requires no pruning but the plants do need shearing back in late autumn or early spring before new growth begins. Stem cuttings root readily in spring or summer.

The catalogue of Thompson & Morgan, the English seed company that also operates in America, offers seeds of 'Gentian Blue', a cultivar of *A. linifolia*, which is itself a subspecies of *A. monelli*, as a half-hardy perennial to be treated as a half-hardy annual. It appears to be virtually the same plant as 'Pacific Blue' and is suggested as an annual ground cover.

ARDISIA

Northern gardeners may know the coralberry, *Ardisia crenata*, as a houseplant having shiny, leathery, evergreen leaves and white flowers in spring followed by long-lasting berries that are a shiny bright red at Christmas. Presumably because it grows so slowly, this small shrub from Malaysia and China remains a minor entity in the commercial world, a fact that to aficionados makes it all the more attractive for nurturing in a private garden indoors, or outdoors where minimum temperatures won't fall more than a few degress below freezing. A relative, the marlberry, *A. japonica*, is shorter in stature, to 12 inches, and grows more quickly, by means of stolon roots. It is also hardier, to around 0°F. or U.S.D.A. Zone 6.

My introduction to *A. japonica* was through the catalogue of

BERRIES ON *ARDISIA JAPONICA*, SHOWN HERE IN THE LONG ISLAND GREENHOUSE OF C. Z. GUEST, ARE LIPSTICK RED. POTTED SPECIMENS ARE AT PEAK COLOR FOR THE CHRISTMAS HOLIDAYS.

ARUNDO

There are two giant reeds that inhabit wetlands or low-lying areas such as roadside ditches, *Phragmites australis* (or *P. communis*) and *Arundo donax*. In *Ornamental Grasses*, a handbook from the Brooklyn Botanic Garden, gardener and photographer Pamela Harper likens the giant reeds to Dr. Jekyll and Mr. Hyde, because although they are quite invasive in wet soils, they are apt to die in dry soils. Among the numerous variants is one with variegated leaves, *A. d.* 'Versicolor'. The plant reminds Harper of sweet corn with white-edged leaves striped in cream and green. The plain green species has naturalized from Zone 7 south and is planted deliberately for a multitude of purposes. It is used as a means of controlling soil erosion as well as for the production of reeds used in musical instruments and the making of wattlework. This species can grow to an impressive height of 20 feet. The smaller 'Versicolor', reaching a height of about ten feet, is rated winter-hardy in Zones 8 to 10. This cultivar can bring grace and beauty to almost any style landscape, whether formal or informal. 'Versicolor' is a superb accent plant, both as a single clump a few feet in diameter and as a colony covering a hundred square feet or more. Cuttings of fresh growth are popular for use in floral arrangements of any style: traditional, Japanese, or contemporary.

Phragmites grows just about everywhere, a veritable vegetable cosmopolite. *Phragmites australis*, growing to nearly 20 feet, is used for making latticework, but more likely to be encountered is its subspecies *australis*, which reaches to 12 feet. All of these plants, whether tall or not-so-tall, plain or variegated, can be aggressive. Try to employ them in such a way as to make this an asset, and so avoid a hostile takeover of the backyard. They are also herbaceous and thus benefit from an annual cutting-back in spring, to make way for new growth.

Logee's Greenhouses (see Resources), which describes it as a "... low growing plant with tufts of glossy green leaves. The tiny pink flowers produce bright red berries." This sounded like something a friend of mine would enjoy in her greenhouse so I gave her one. It has turned out to be a splendid potted specimen that spends summers outdoors in a slathouse and winters in a frost-free sun pit, except when it is doing duty as a decorative pot plant indoors.

Last spring, however, I saw *A. japonica* in a new light, employed as evergreen ground cover under an enormous shade tree at Live Oak Gardens in Louisiana. There it interlaced in one area with holly ferns, *Cyrtomium falcatum*, in another with flowering impatiens. *The Good Housekeeping Illustrated Encyclopedia of Gardening* says ardisia "... is suitable for a deep ground cover in peaty woodlands," noting that at least five forms are grown in Japan, some having white or pink variegated leaves.

THE STRIPED GIANT REED, *ARUNDO DONAX* 'VERSICOLOR', IS BEAUTIFUL IN THE LANDSCAPE UP CLOSE OR AT SOME DISTANCE.

AVENA

Blue oatgrass, *Avena sempervirens*, also known as *Helictotrichon sempervirens*, is similar in color and appearance to blue fescue but taller, with a firmer conformation. It is hardy in Zones 4 to 8 and grows to about 12 inches tall, a little more in bloom. The habit of the plant is tufted, with the central leaves growing rather definitely straight up, the outer leaves arching gracefully. The erect panicles of straw-colored flowers appear in summer.

As grasses go, this one has a surprising tolerance — if not a need for — sandy, well-drained soil. Grow it in sun as a single accent plant, in small groups toward the front of a perennial border or in a rock garden, or in masses as a full-fledged ground cover. Wait to cut back blue oat grass until earliest spring, at which time the winter-weary tussocks may be sheared back to an inch or so above the soil. In a matter of weeks after the arrival of frost-free, increasingly warm weather, they will be decked out in new silvery blue leaves.

AVENA SEMPERVIRENS (above) IS IN THE FOREGROUND. *CALAMAGROSTIS* IS A HANDSOME BACKGROUND FOR *RUDBECKIA FULGIDA* 'GOLDSTURM' (below). SEDGES ARE FEATURED AT LIVE OAK GARDENS (opposite).

BOUTELOUA

Bouteloua is a genus of about fifty species from the central United States to Argentina, including side-oats grama, *B. curtipendula*, blue grama, *B. gracilis*, hairy grama, *B. hirsuta*, and slender grama, *B. repens*. The gramas are essential in gardens of prairie grasses and have recently come under consideration for more ornamental gardens as well. The drought-tolerant gramas are also valuable in Xeriscaping and are being used increasingly in gardens of native plants. They may be used as single specimen plants, grouped or massed, or in the company of such sun-loving wild flowers as blanket flower, *Gaillardia*, and Kansas gay-feather, *Liatris pychostachya*.

CALAMAGROSTIS

Feather reed grass, *Calamagrostis acutiflora* 'Stricta', grows five to seven feet tall, is winter hardy in Zones 5 to 9, and best planted in groups in a sunny spot. The form in profile is upright, arching, and narrow. According to White Flower Farm, this hybrid occurred naturally in Europe and has become popular in cultivated gardens for its pale, feathery flowers that open at the height of summer, then age gracefully from soft cream to warm brown, and finally to silvery gray in winter. This grass may be displayed in a dried arrangement in a vase, or included as a flower border backdrop, scattered informally over a bank, or planted in more ordered, even modular, groupings. If any grass has ever gotten away from you, to the point of being a weed, possibly the most important thing to know about feather reed grass is that it is a clump-forming, sterile hybrid that slowly expands to three feet in diameter but essentially stays where it has been planted.

The cultivar *C. arundinacea* is a foot or so shorter than the species, and has attractive pinkish purple, feathery blooms in early to midsummer. Its stiff reedy stems will stand erect through snow. During the growing season, the leaves are dark green. Calamagrostis is one of the ornamental grasses associated with the work of Washington, D.C.-based landscape architects Wolfgang Oehme and James van Sweden, who often plant it in the company of such plants as *Rudbeckia fulgida* 'Goldsturm', *Sedum spectabile* 'Autumn Joy', and Russian sage, *Perovskia atriplicifolia*. These grow, interact, and sometimes bloom together in an Oehme/van Sweden garden at the University of Minnesota School of Business.

Another perennial ornamental grass in the genus is Korean reed grass, *C.* × *arundinacea brachytricha*, which is hardy in Zones 6 to 9. It grows only two to three feet tall, is upright, arching, and narrow in profile.

CAREX

The sedges grow on their own as ground covers everywhere, and some certain of them have been encouraged to live as part of cultivated gardens. *Carex morrowi* 'Aureo variegata', variegated Japanese sedge, has slender, grassy, drooping leaves of bright cream, to 18 inches tall, with dark green stripes along the edges. It is semi-evergreen, hardy in Zones 5 to 9, and fares best in moist partial shade. *Carex conica* 'Hime-Kan-suge',

hardy in Zones 6 to 9, and at most four inches high, forms a symmetrical rosette of dark green leaves that have a narrow white stripe along the edges.

The sedges, including the genus *Cyperus* (*C. papyrus*, the papyrus of the ancient world, also known as bulrush, and *C. alternifolius*, the umbrella-plant), are grass-like; unlike the true grasses, which have leaves that are round in cross section, the leaves of sedges are triangular. The rushes, also grass-like plants, in the genus *Juncus*, have wiry stems with thin basal leaves and small numbers of onion-like flowers at the top.

CAREX, CYPERUS, AND ACORUS GROW WITH
"WATER BABY" AT ATLANTA BOTANICAL GARDEN
(left). VARIEGATED CAREX (above) HAS A WHITE
STRIPE DOWN THE CENTER OF EACH LEAF. WILD
GRASSES AND SEDGES (below) ARE POTTED FROM
THE GARDENER'S PROPERTY.

CHRYSANTHEMUM

Cynical horticulturists have been known to dismiss the chrysanthemum as entirely too utilitarian to be of interest, but the genus *Chrysanthemum* is rich in plants cherished by specialty growers who may in turn give them a variety of different botanical names. Boston daisy, for example, once called *C. frutescens* 'Chrysaster' and before that *Anthemis frutescens*, is now considered part of the genus *Argyranthemum*. (It is fortunate that changing the name of a plant in no way alters the care it needs, otherwise gardeners would be hopelessly confused.)

Chrysanthemum ptarmicifolium is very different in appearance from the more familiar species; this one is a low plant with feathery silver foliage that forms a cushion to six inches high. In a sunny site having light and well-drained soil, hardly any of the garden's silver-leaved plants are as exquisitely cut as this elegantly refined Chrysanthemum. *Chrysanthemum parthenium* 'Aureum' gives a similar appearance but in glowing golden green, with white daisy flowers in late summer to autumn. It is grown as an annual, often under the trade name *Pyrethrum parthenifolium* 'Aureum'. When growing the plants primarily for foliage effect, remove flower buds as early as possible.

CYMBOPOGON

Lemongrass, *Cymbopogon citratus*, has been known to herbalists as "fever grass." These days it is something of a darling among the gourmet, health food, and beverage crowd. Originally from southern India and Ceylon, lemongrass is widely cultivated in the Tropics. Elsewhere it makes an entirely satisfactory container plant, moved outdoors during frost-free weather, and brought inside in winter, when it need only be kept above freezing and on the dry side.

An established root division planted in well-drained soil in a sawed-off whiskey barrel at the beginning of the growing season by midsummer will become a dense clump up to six

CHRYSANTHEMUM PTARMICIFOLIUM IS A VERY HARDY AND VERY FINELY CUT-LEAVED DUSTY MILLER (left). FOR GROUND COVER OR BORDER EDGING, WITH SILVER FILIGREE EFFECT.

feet tall, comprised of slender three-foot green leaves. Lemongrass seldom flowers but is grown for its graceful appearance, the rustling sound of the leaves in gentle breezes, and of course the smell and taste. Water freely in warm weather.

Citronellagrass, *Cymbopogon nardus*, the source of citronella oil, is cultivated in the tropics as well as southern Florida and southern California. Like lemongrass, this species grows most actively in warm weather and needs well-drained, humus-rich soil. Both species can be cut to an inch or so from the ground in early spring, and can be divided and replanted at the same time. They are virtually impervious to insect, disease, or any other problems; the presence of citronellagrass helps to repel mosquitoes from the garden.

ERIANTHUS RAVENNAE

I doubt there breathes a northern gardener who is not impressed or possibly quite smitten on first meeting a well-grown clump of pampas grass in full plume. Better yet is a roadside planting along a freeway cloverleaf that features a dramatic sweep of many clumps of pampas grass. The plants are somehow more graceful than referring to them as "clumps" makes them sound. However, some gardeners find the rigid flower stalks unappealing and there are even a few people who have no use at all for this classic ornamental grass from Latin America. Those who do admire pampas grass but live where winters are too cold for it can take solace in ravenna grass, more properly *Erianthus ravennae*.

Originally from southern Europe, ravenna grass is winter hardy to around 0°F., and can reach 14 feet tall in a single season. In autumn the slender canes are crowned by silvery purple spikelets. Even in winter, after hard frost has browned and shrunken the ravenna, it still stands and can be at its most beautiful as a warm sun starts to melt the ice that has crystallized on its leaves. A commanding clump of ravenna grass anchors one end of a large free-form bed of grasses and other monocotyledons at the Brooklyn Botanic Garden. Although it changes color from season to season, and may even slump a little in the winter, ravenna grass keeps its essential architectural form all through the year — except when new shoots are developing after the plants are cut back in spring. It needs sun and well-drained but fertile and moist soil.

It can get on with a lot of other plants, at least culturally speaking. In terms of design, I suggest thinking of ravenna grass as a very large ground cover. It might be used in a grouping of three or *en masse* over quite a large area. Think big. A so-so perennial border could shape up with ravenna grass used as accents.

THIS PHOTOGRAPH OF HARDY RAVENNA GRASS, *ERIANTHUS RAVENNAE*, WAS TAKEN IN DECEMBER AT BROOKLYN BOTANIC GARDEN, WHERE IT DOMINATES ONE END OF A FREE-FORM BED. THE RAVENNA CAN GO TO 12 FEET IN A SINGLE SEASON AND IS ALWAYS ATTRACTIVE.

FESTUCA

HOUTTUYNIA

While pampas grass has long been popular in warmer and Mediterranean climates, it is the blue fescue that perhaps more than any other ornamental grass has influenced the way today's gardener looks upon such plants. The myriad new gardens that sprouted up in California after World War II often featured clumps of blue fescue set out geometrically, so that each tufted plant remained separate and distinct from the others. The effect was photogenic even in an era when black-and-white photography predominated. Shelter magazines such as *Sunset* and *House Beautiful* were quick to promote the use of blue fescue, known first in the trade as *Festuca glauca*, later in *Hortus Third* as

BLUE FESCUE (left) SURROUNDS *PANICUM VIRGATUM* WITH *COREOPSIS VERTICILLATA* 'MOONBEAM'. 'CHAMELEON' (right) IS A HOUTTUYNIA THAT NEEDS LOTS OF SUNLIGHT.

F. ovina var. *glauca*, now as *F. caesia* by ornamental grass authority Roger Grounds, and as either of two cultivars belonging to *F. cinerea*, 'Superba' and 'Blausilber', by United States grower and Grammarian (for an expert on Gramineae, the Grass Family), Kurt Bluemel.

Today as always, the blue fescue looks best as an isolated specimen, no matter whether it is surrounded by other plants exactly the same or entirely different. The handsome symmetry of a blue fescue plant somehow does not find the same sense of resolution when the distinct and regular outline is blurred or intruded upon. Alone or massed, blue fescue can be used in rectangular or curving beds, in Western or Japanese-style landscapes. The number of different names attributed to this grass in recent times reflects its popularity. It looks good next to other grasses, perennials, and conifers.

The listing for *Houttuynia* (who-TEEN-ee-uh) in *The American Horticultural Society Encyclopedia of Garden Plants* notes that it represents a one-species genus, a deciduous, marginal water plant having "far spreading rhizomes." In other words, the plant can be invasive. It can also be an attractive ground cover in Zones 5 to 9, for a place that is semisunny to semishady and constantly moist or boggy, such as beside a stream.

All of the houttuynias appear in the systematic collection at the Brooklyn Botanic Garden. Besides the plain green-leaved *H. cordata*, to 15 inches tall with single white flowers, there is *H. c.* 'Flore Pleno', with double white flowers and plain green leaves. *Houttuynia cordata* 'Chameleon' has yellow- and red-splashed leaves, the coloring of which is enhanced by more direct sun. Recently introduced from Korea, 'Chameleon' is only six to nine inches tall. Plantsman John Elsley notes that it is excellent for container culture. The heart-shaped leaves and tidy habit could look wonderful in a bonsai pot or tray.

MISCANTHUS

The Asian Miscanthus is universally praised for fountain-of-grass effects in summer, a glorious time of flowering in autumn, for its use in dried arrangements, and for its hardiness. The upright open form and relative tallness suggest solo plantings or small groupings thrusting through low ground cover, or massing as screens. A sunny location and deep, moist soil foster the densest growth for screening.

Slender maiden grass, *Miscanthus sinensis* 'Gracillimus', has leaves hardly a quarter-inch wide, gray-green with a highlighting white midrib. The plumes, five to six feet high, open burgundy, age to soft pink, and pass the winter as buff. Narrow variegated maiden grass forms a fountain up to five feet high of finely textured green leaves banded narrowly in white along the edges; the effect is silvery green, luminous, and shimmering, entirely appropriate for the cultivar name 'Morning Light'. 'Silver Feather' ('Silberpfeder'), or *M. s. condensatus*, blooms several weeks earlier than most miscanthus, with medium-wide leaves and plumes carried to two feet above the foliage mass. The flower plumes open pale gold and darken to silken magenta, inspiring the name "purple-blooming Japanese silver grass". Its mature height is six to eight feet. Zebra grass, *M. s.* 'Zebrinus', has transverse bands of creamy yellow across its leaves, making it, to my mind, one of the more exotic looking of cultivated plants.

MISCANTHUS SINENSIS 'ZEBRINUS' INSPIRES THOUGHTS OF EXOTIC, FAR-AWAY PLACES.

PENNISETUM

Fountain grass is *Pennisetum setaceum*, known variously in the seed trade as *P. ruppelianum* and *P. ruppelii*. It grows to about three and one-half feet high, including the showy inflorescence that is pink or purplish and up to a foot long. An extensive planting of fountain grass juxtaposed with pink wax begonias in beds along an allée at Longwood Gardens in Pennsylvania has favorably impressed hundreds of thousands of visitors. In addition to the species there are also the cultivars 'Atrosanguineum', 'Burgundy Giant', and 'Cupreum' (which all have purple leaves and spikes), and 'Rubrum' (with rosy leaves and spikes), which look beautiful in the company of almost all flowers, annual or perennial, in full sun. Chinese pennisetum or rose fountain grass, *P. alopecuroides*, is also cultivated and, unlike the others, is winter-hardy to below 0°F.

Most of the fountain grasses are treated as annuals except in the warmest climates, where they are perennial. Seeds germinate in three weeks at 70°F. At the other end of the season, in milder regions, it is important not to let the seeds fall, or self-sown seedlings could become a problem. In cold climates the seedheads can be left standing for their effect in the winter landscape.

Any of these pennisetums can make a wonderful showing when grown in a fairly large container, approximately the size of a bushel, alone or with smaller plants around the base. The fountain grasses are widely planted in gardens and as embankment or hillside ground covers in drier parts of the Deep South for, once established, they are drought-tolerant.

POLYGONUM CUSPIDATUM SPREADS ITS BRANCHES AT LONGWOOD GARDENS (right). THE BAMBOO-LIKE STALKS HAVE BEEN TRAINED TO FORM A FANCIFUL TRUNK AND TREE SHAPE.

POLYGONUM CUSPIDATUM

There is a place in Connecticut where a semi-abandoned farmyard, with assorted piles of machinery and junk in various stages of rust or rot, becomes nearly completely covered over between spring and autumn by Mexican bamboo, also known as Japanese knotweed *Polygonum cuspidatum*. Species from the same genus may be encountered on almost any walk through New York's Central Park. And there is a handsome stand of Mexican bamboo that grows every summer in High Falls,

New York, rising up between a concrete culvert and a building foundation.

Since this is a plant that itself seems to get up and walk around, I was surprised to see it in the herbaceous borders at Longwood Gardens. There, individual clumps are kept from spreading by a root barrier in the soil; instead, the green 'bamboo' stems form a dense column about two feet in diameter and four or five feet tall. The stems are crowned by a leafy, tree-like mass of leaves. In the company of miscanthus grass and annual and perennial flowers, the effect is most unusual.

In the right place, which is to say sunny, boggy, acidic, and neither too cold, nor too hot, or without any cold at all (meaning roughly Zones 7 to 9), nothing could be a more extraordinary ground cover than one or more species or hybrids (natural or man-made) from the insectivorous genus *Sarracenia*.

could be *S. flava* (found from Virginia to Florida and Alabama). If purple, the plants could be common pitcher plant, *S. purpurea*, which is distributed in eastern North America in acid bogs as far north as Zone 3 (although survival in cold is tied in with dormancy and being covered with water at the

At the time the photograph here was being taken at the Atlanta Botanical Garden on an afternoon in late April, numerous other photographers were also at work, each with a different vision. Each photographer was trying to express the experience of being in the midst of a whole crowd of pitcher plants; are they all the same, or all different? If yellow they

time of freeze-up). Others include *S. minor* (with clear yellow flowers to two and a half inches across, and native from North Carolina to Florida), *S. psittacina* (red-purple flowers to two inches; Georgia and Florida to Louisiana), and *S. rubra* (maroon flowers to one and a half inches across; North Carolina to Florida and Mississippi).

TRITICUM

Triticum spelta, Spelt wheat, grows to 24 inches tall and has an effective flowering period of four to six weeks in the garden. Durum or bearded wheat, *T. turgidum*, is the same size or somewhat taller, and has the same flowering period. Its long seeds, unique among plants in the Grass Family, have bristles that give them a bearded appearance. The flower stalks are a delightful addition to flower arrangements, fresh or dried. Its seeds germinate readily after ten to twenty days in warm and moist conditions. The tradition of cultivating this hardy annual reaches far back in time. Because of its resistance to drought, durum wheat is grown in most arid regions of the world. Its seeds are ground to become durum flour.

Several cultivars of *Triticum aestrivum* are offered in the catalogue of The Country Garden (see Resources). The catalogue describes them as "wild cousins of edible wheats, with long, showy bristles (awns), giving a most rustic look." 'Pelissier Black Tip' is an antique wheat brought from Algeria in 1929 and favored by Saskatchewan wheat-weavers. 'Black Knight' grows to five feet and is sown in fall; it has a dark blue-black color throughout the head and awns. 'Black Eagle' is a spring-seeded type growing two to three feet, with almost all-black heads and awns. 'Black Tip', also spring-seeded, reaches two to three feet, with white heads and black awns. 'Silver Tip' grows two to three feet, is spring-seeded, and produces extra-large all white heads. Another wheat to grow is einkorn wheat, *T. monococcum*, which dates from the Stone Age. It reaches a height of 40 inches, with small, fine stems, thin and wiry, and slender, pale red flower spikes one to three inches long, flattened and bearded. Einkorn wheat is an ancient plant that could be rediscovered as a garden ornamental, dried for artistic purpose, or harvested and ground for use by the home baker.

SARRACENIAS GROW *EN MASSE* IN A SUNNY, ACIDIC BOG AT THE ATLANTA BOTANICAL GARDEN (opposite), BLOOMING IN LATE APRIL. THESE INSECTIVOROUS PLANTS ARE NATIVE NORTH AMERICANS THAT ARE CONSIDERED CHOICE WHEREVER A GARDENER IS ABLE TO SUPPLY THEIR NEEDS, INCLUDING AN AMPLE DIET OF INSECTS.

WINTER AND SPRING WHEATS (above) ARE GARDEN WORTHY, BOTH ORNAMENTAL AND EDIBLE. THEY ARE AVAILABLE IN NUMEROUS COLORS AND COMBINATIONS, SOME DATING FROM THE STONE AGE. FULL SUN AND WELL-DRAINED SOIL ARE REQUIRED, ALONG WITH ADEQUATE MOISTURE UNTIL THE ROOTS ARE DEEPLY ESTABLISHED.

CHAPTER
SEVEN

THE
COLOR
GARDEN

Of all the ingredients that make a garden beautiful, color is among the more elusive. Recently in the New York Times, garden editor Anne Raver cited the planting of "garish orange something-or-others next to pink ones" as being one of the classic mistakes made by beginners. Well, I happen to like orange and pink flowers together. The theme of this chapter is more about foliage colors, however, and nothing holds still about them — they change by the hour and by the season on the same plant in the same garden. To bring some order from the apparent chaos, I will look at foliage color in three subsections, as silver blue, red-burgundy and golden-yellow. ❧ The 'Blue Daze' evolvulus illustrated here has flowers so blue that they will heighten the effect of any blue-tinted leaf placed in the same visual context. The silvery quality of the evolvulus foliage is less obvious, however, and can be brought out by the juxtaposition of a plant whose leaves are strongly silver but of a different texture or scale, such as lamb's-ears (Stachys byzantina) or the lacy, sweet-smelling Artemisia 'Powis Castle'. Conversely, both the silver and the blue of the evolvulus can be enhanced by placing it in the company of dwarf blue fescue. ❧ Another use of color is the pattern garden such as the one shown on the preceding pages at Mohonk Mountain House in New Paltz, New York. Individually none of these plants is all that interesting, but when they are planted together in careful patterns, laced around each other, in arcs and right angles, so that some of the lines appear to be woven under, then over others, the plants take on the intrigue of a knot garden or parterre. ❧ Color intensity is affected by latitude and weather conditions. In the tropics, intense sunlight burns off colors, so they are seen as less vivid. Conversely, colors appear brighter under cloudy skies, which may explain why subtly variegated plants are popular in England, the Pacific Northwest, and other areas known for overcast weather.

❧ In the world of plants, silver is more valuable than gold, possibly because it goes as well with cool colors as with hot ones. Silver plants also have a luminosity at dusk and in the moonlight that imbues them with a certain romance or even otherworldliness.

❧ When it is time to match one color foliage with another, or with a flower, or even with the paint trim of one's house, nothing beats taking a leaf or two of one plant from here and a blossom of that plant from over there and trying them out together in reading-quality light. When going shopping for plants, take leaf and flower samples from home, in a recloseable plastic bag with a splash of water. No matter what the plant or the place, color carries emotional power. In the garden, use the colors of one's own preference, and remember: Massing color makes a greater impact than mixing.

SANTOLINA HEDGES (previous pages) DETAIL BEDS OF *ALTERNANTHERA* AND BEGONIAS. *EVOLVULUS GLOMERATUS* (opposite) IS A BUSH MORNING-GLORY.

SILVER BLUE

AJUGA REPTANS ARGENTEA 'KINGWOOD' SPREADS ITS SILVER LEAVES IN SUMMER AT THE
BASE OF A HYDRANGEA QUERCIFOLIA 'SNOW QUEEN' IN THE GARDEN OF SALLY REATH.

AJUGA 'KINGWOOD'

Plain green bugleweed, *Ajuga reptans*, a European native, has naturalized in the eastern United States and may be hardly noticed except when the spikes of bluish purple flowers appear above the carpet of foliage in spring. Bugleweed is hardy to Zone 3 and even where covered in winter by snow, remains evergreen. Or not-so-green, for the species is delightfully prone to mutations, among them 'Kingwood', an extra silvery cultivar of the subspecies *argentea*. (The word *argentea* — or *argenteus* — is one way for a taxonomist to indicate that a plant is silvery; others to watch for in a quest for this effect from plants are *cinereus, dealbatus,* and *incanus*.) One way to employ 'Kingwood' is as edging along a path, where it will help guide the way at

ARABIS CAUCASICA 'COCCINEUM' BLOOMS WITH ROSEMARY. THE ARABIS GETS ITS SILVERY APPEARANCE FROM WHITE-MARGINED LEAVES.

dusk or in moonlight. The smooth leaves of 'Kingwood' have a metallic pigmentation that keeps their underlying green from being seen; they will be most silver when in general good health, with perhaps the slightest stress from strong light or not quite enough water.

Bugleweed is a ground cover that gets on well in average conditions — some sun, some shade, and soil that is deeply moist until the roots are well established, after which it can dry out a little. Some other colorful ajugas include *A.r.* 'Variegata' (white-edged leaves), *A.r.* 'Rubra' (purple leaves), *A.r.* 'Atropurpurea' (bronze leaves), *A.r.* 'Metallica Crispa' (curled leaves having a blue cast), 'Burgundy Lace' (reddish burgundy), 'Bronze Beauty' (dark purple), 'Burgundy Glow' (creamy white on green with bold splashes of wine red) and 'Gaiety' (bronze-red leaves streaked with tan, cream, gold, and copper).

ARABIS CAUCASICA

Arabis caucasica is a Mediterranean species hardy to Zone 6. In its cultivar 'Coccineum' the flowers are rose-red and the white-margined leaves give a silvery appearance. Another variegated plant for the rock garden is white-flowered *A. ferdinandi coburgii* 'Variegata', which forms a one-inch-high, spreading mat of tidy, glossy leaves that are bordered in creamy white, but

flushed pink in the cold months; this plant is hardy to Zone 5. One of the rarest is the double white *A. albida* 'Flore Plena', which looks like a miniature stock.

The arabis form large mats of evergreen leaves and are at their best as carpeters in a rockery or spilling from dry walls or over ledges of garden walls. They go all to bloom in earliest spring. All these select varieties must be propagated by division or cuttings in the spring. Arabis are easily grown in a sunny site in well-drained soil. Shear lightly after flowering.

The first begonias having silver-spotted leaves were brought into cultivation in England around 1850, but it was the introduction of *Begonia rex* at this time that caused a horticultural furor in Europe. The English taxonomists saw clearly this was a begonia fit for a king. When gardeners discovered that propagation was possible from the leaves, the royal plants proliferated and soon everyone who fancied their brilliantly ornamental foliage could have them. Helen K. Krauss in her 1947 book, *Begonias for American Homes and Gardens*, notes that leaves of the rexes ". . . are unique in that they assume many of the colors of the rainbow, including certain shades of blue. The base colors are often overlaid with shimmering silver or other colorful metallic lusters." She goes on to note that they are easy to grow, which is true if their growth cycle is understood. It is similar to that of the summer-flowering tuberous begonias. In autumn and winter the plants need to be kept on the dry side and in moderate temperatures. However, in a fluorescent-light garden with four 40-watt tubes operated 16 hours out of every 24, temperatures ranging from 60° to 75°F., and 50 percent or more relative humidity, the rexes can be kept in fine form all year.

The leaf of a rex begonia can be rooted exactly like that of an African violet, *Saintpaulia*, with about a half-inch of the petiole (leaf stalk) inserted in the rooting medium. A cluster of begonia babies exactly like the parent will arise. An even more remarkable technique is to cut through the main veins on the underside of a mature rex leaf using a razor-sharp knife; lay cut side down on a clean, moist rooting medium. Press lightly in place, mist with tepid water, then enclose in glass or plastic. Baby plants will arise from each cut made in a main vein. Seeds of rex begonias yield plants with a mix of leaf colors. Besides the large-leaved rexes, which form plants to 18 inches in diameter and as tall, there are miniatures a third this size.

BEGONIA REX

CERTAIN REX BEGONIAS HAVE A METALLIC SILVER COLOR ON THE LEAF'S UPPER SURFACE THAT SEEMS MORE MINERAL THAN VEGETABLE.

DYCKIA FOSTERANA

DYCKIA FOSTERANA GIVES THE IMPRESSION OF
SILVER FROM THE LEAVES' TINY MOISTURE-
GATHERING STRUCTURES.

Silver and gold dyckia, *Dyckia fosterana*, is singularly noteworthy, in part because it is one of the species deemed outstanding enough to bear the name of the person who put bromeliads on the map, Mulford B. Foster. Unlike the currently popular florist bromeliads that are epiphytes, the dyckia is a xerophytic terrestrial whose original home was on South American campos or growing on rocks. Foster discovered in a remote spot in Parana, Brazil, the plant that was to be named in his honor. Late in life he was gleeful that when other plant hunters had asked him where he found *fosterana*, the instructions he provided for retracing his steps were always missing one vital turn. This was not due to meanness but rather a protective attitude toward the plants themselves and Foster's belief that the thrill of the hunt would be diminished if it were too easy.

A well-grown *D. fosterana* produces a robust, whorled rosette of stiff silvery purple leaves, the margins prominently silver-spined, and, when mature, a spike of intense orange flowers. The silver appearance comes primarily from the tiny, moisture-gathering scale structures that occur over most of the leaf surface in this species of bromeliad, and in bands or stripes in others, such as *Billbergia zebrina* or zebra urn, a related but epiphytic bromeliad. Somewhat more easily managed as houseplants than dyckia, in sunny to bright windows or in a four-tube fluorescent-light garden, are the earth-star bromeliads, members of the terrestrial genus *Cryptanthus*. These are noteworthy for being striped, cross-banded, or mottled in silver over a base color that may be green, bronze, or burgundy-purplish. In *Cryptanthus fosteranus* the coppery green to purplish brown leaves have silvery tan zebra cross-banding. While nature has provided about twenty different species of *Cryptanthus*, breeders have produced many more, especially from Germany in recent years. In all cases, bromeliads in cultivation do well along with orchids, gesneriads, and aroids. Each shoot or rosette of leaves blooms once, usually when one to two years of age.

LAMIASTRUM

Lamiastrum, Lamium, and *Galeobdolon* are all names applied to creeping, trailing or decumbent members of the Mint Family. The best of them are noteworthy for some of the most silver leaves in the vegetable kingdom, and cold hardy in Zones 3 to 9. *Lamiastrum galeobdolon* 'Variegatum' (also called *Galeobdolon argentatum*) has silver-marked green leaves and yellow flowers in spring. Its stems root where the nodes come in contact with moist soil. A dwarf form, 'Compactum', has half-inch leaves and grows to only six inches. The mound-forming cultivars 'Hansen's Variety' (notable for silver speckling on the leaves and a neat habit) and 'Herman's Pride' (small silver-variegated leaves) are recommended.

The genus *Lamium,* spotted dead nettle, is now sometimes referred to as *Lamiastrum.* By either name, *L. maculatum* is exceptionally endowed with the trait of silver foliage and evergreen — eversilver to be more precise — growth. 'Beacon Silver' is one of the stars of the species, an acclaimed ground cover that does best with plenty of shade through midday. It has silver-white leaves with a thin green margin on decumbent plants six to eight inches tall, but spreads to cover an area several times this in diameter. There are dark pink flowers in spring. 'Silver Sweet' has green-veined silver leaves that are toothed at the edges and a profusion of lemon yellow flowers. 'White Nancy' is similar to 'Beacon Silver,' but has white flowers and more spreading habit. It looks splendid in a bed with white-variegated hosta and *Liriope muscari* 'Munroe White'.

LAMIASTRUM 'BEACON SILVER' (opposite) IS AN ENERGETIC PERENNIAL GROUND COVER DISTINGUISHED BY GREEN-MARGINED, SILVER-WHITE LEAVES. *LAMIASTRUM* 'SILVER CARPET' (left) GIVES A MOSAIC OF GREEN AND SILVER.

PHILODENDRON

Silver, pewter, and blue are colors or sheens often seen in the leaves of aroids, including *Philodendron*, *Scindapsus*, and *Epipremnum*. Blueness is primarily from a smooth, glaucous or waxy coating that prevents the green of the leaf from being seen. A current catalogue from Glasshouse Works (see Resources) lists the following candidates for this color class: *Philodendron andreanum* × *sodiroi* (velvety, heart-shaped leaves of mottled emerald and gray pewter), *P. bipennifolium* 'Glaucous' (waxy bluish gray fiddle-shaped leaves), *P. glaucaphyllum* blue fiddleleaf philodendron (aluminum-silver to blue over a waxy undertone), an unidentified species from Iquiotos, Ecuador (with glossy blue-pewter leaves), and *P. ornatum* (bluish green margins on silver

leaves; formerly called *P. sodiroi*). A related plant is the satin pothos, *Scindapsus pictus* 'Argyraeus', a much-loved houseplant with satiny, heart-shaped leaves that are bluish green with silvery markings and margins. The amazingly blue cutleaf *Epipremnum* shown in the photograph is an unidentified species from the Phillipines that is in the collection of Florida plantsman Jean Merkel.

VINCA MINOR

Trailing myrtle or periwinkle (named for the color of its flowers) is one of the all-time greats among evergreen ground covers. It does best in shade but the leaves are such a dark green they can hardly be seen in the shadows. The solution is to plant one of the variegated varieties. *Vinca minor* 'Argenteo-variegata' or 'Sterling Silver' has white-edged leaves, while in 'Variegata' or 'Aureo-variegata' they are creamy-margined. In ei-ther case the individual leaves appear to have been highlighted; as a result the plant is effective in the landscape instead of merely a serviceable ground cover that is taken for granted but never really appreciated for its special effects.

Another cultivar having colorful variegation is 'Aureola,' with creamy yellow veins through the center of its leaves. Other vincas noteworthy for differences in habit or flower color from that of *V. minor* are 'Flore Pleno' (double wine-red flowers), 'Purpurea' (purplish red flowers), 'La Grave' or 'Bowles Variety' (a super race of *V. minor*, with broader, waxier leaves, and larger, darker blue flowers), and 'Miss Jekyll' (a white-flowered dwarf, for small areas).

RED BURGUNDY

BASELLA ALBA

BASELLA ALBA (above), IS A HOT-WEATHER
SUBSTITUTE FOR TRUE SPINACH. COLEUS
(opposite), HERE IN C.Z. GUEST'S GREENHOUSE
JUST BEFORE PLANTING-OUT TIME, COMES IN
PERSIAN CARPET COLORS.

Malabar spinach is another name for *Basella alba*, a fast-growing warm-weather substitute for spinach that also makes an ornamental vine. Train it to a fence or on substantial tepees six to eight feet tall and, particularly in the South, allow generous space as it can become massive in a matter of weeks. Start harvesting the young violet-purple tips about two months after planting and use them like Popeye spinach, steamed lightly or raw in salads.

A cultivar called 'Red Stem' has been grown recently at EPCOT Center in Florida's Disney World, and its presence there has created considerable interest in what one seed company terms a "delicious new vegetable from the Orient". Not to quibble over the "new", but *B. alba* 'Rubra', which sounds the same as 'Red Stem' with reddish stems, petioles and flowers, was written up in *Hortus Third*. Of course, until a new plant is grown well and displayed where would-be growers can see the merits, it can remain obscure.

Be advised that basella, like okra, is a plant that doesn't just tolerate hot weather; in fact, it longs for the sort of days that keep humans next to the air conditioner. To achieve the best growth, coloration, and flavor, start with deeply spaded soil that has been enriched with well-rotted compost. Be sure to maintain fairly deep soil moisture in the early stages of growth, in order to encourage the roots to grow deep. That way, when midsummer dryness comes along, the plants will be more self-reliant. At this time it will also help to apply a three- to four-inch mulch of organic matter to the soil.

Basella is one of those fast-growing summer vines that makes a great coverup for children's playhouses. The heart-shaped green leaves are beautiful, especially because they are threaded together by such brilliantly colored stems.

COLEUS

Among plants having leaves in colors other than green, hardly any equal *Coleus* for shades of red, burgundy, purple, and pink (not to mention the family of chartreuse, cream, yellow, and salmon). Most of the coleus grown are hybrids developed from *C. blumei*, a Javanese native introduced in England in 1853. 'Pineapple Beauty', which first appeared in an 1877 catalogue, is still trained the world over as a tree-form standard. The strongly upright habit and relatively large leaves of 'Pineapple Beauty' represent one class of today's coleus.

The best plants are formed when they are pinched frequently during the early stages of growth. They are also as a class easier to train into tree-form standards, usually ranging from 30 to 48 inches tall. The development of a tree requires approximately one year, from the time a single-stemmed seedling or cutting is set in a pot with a stake of the height the trunk is to be. Pinch out all side growths until the main growth shoot reaches the top of the stake. At this point, pinch out the main shoot. Two branches will form and when each has two sets of leaves, pinch out the tip. Continue this practice until the tree head has the size and shape desired.

Although no introduction date is known, another classic coleus is 'Red Mars' or 'Purple Duckfoot', a nonblooming plant that branches from the base and reliably forms without special training individual compact globes of reddish purple to coppery pink leaves.

Some of today's most up-to-date seed strains have the base-branching habit, which makes them more appealing to busy gardeners and to professionals whose bottom-line constraints prevent the time-consuming activity of pinching back hundreds or thousands of plants, such as those seen in the lavish beds at Disney World. In all cases, coleus colors are brightest with fairly high light intensities but not burning sun.

HEMIGRAPHIS ALTERNATA

Red ivy, *Hemigraphis alternata*, is not related to English ivy but is rather a member of the Acanthus Family, probably from the eastern part of the Malay Archipelago. It is a prostrate plant that roots as it grows along the ground and produces a dense cover of three-inch, metallic silver leaves that are red on the underside. Red ivy does best in fairly high temperatures, accompanied by moist, fresh circulating air and strong light, but

with protection from hot, direct sun through midday. Grow red ivy as a houseplant in a hanging basket, or use it for bedding-out in warm weather. The photograph was taken in the gardens at the Governor's palace in Old San Juan, Puerto Rico, in August.

'Exotica Variegata' has yellow splotches in metallic purple leaves. A miniature, 'Red Equator', forms a tidy mat of grape-sized, silver-and-purple leaves. These plants have small, white flowers but are never known to produce seeds, so they are multiplied exclusively from cuttings, ideally in late winter or early spring in a warm, bright, moist place.

PERILLA

Perilla is an old-fashioned plant that self-sows in a pleasant sort of way; meaning it comes back on its own but not so aggressively that it could be called a weed. Perilla is also one of those plants that keeps making a comeback as "new," and sometimes as a "new vegetable from the Orient." Of course, if you have never seen the perilla or even heard of it, then for you it is definitely "new."

Perilla frutescens is grown in Japan and eastern Asia for its oil-bearing seeds. An erect annual, to three feet, it has greenish or purplish leaves, broadly heart-shaped and up to five inches long. In the cultivar 'Atropurpurea' the leaves are dark purple and in 'Crispa' they are narrowly lobed and toothed, marginally

LEAVES OF *HEMIGRAPHIS ALTERNATA* (left) ARE SILVER METALLIC ON TOP, BURGUNDY BENEATH. PURPLE PERILLA AND BRONZE FENNEL (opposite) MAKE A HIGHLY SOPHISTICATED DUO.

wrinkled, and usually purple or bronze, occasionally streaked with bright green. There is also a plain green form of *P. frutescens*.

Another name for this plant is *shiso*, which refers to its use in Asian cooking. A Chinese friend says that the young tips are delicious in mixed stir-fries with other herbs and vegetables. I find the taste a bit piquant but also have a hunch that it will grow on me, in the same way that cilantro or Chinese parsley has changed from something distasteful to one of my favorite garnishes. Most gardeners grow perilla for the color and quilting of the leaves. The plants are at home in any garden, with flowers, vegetables, or in a bed of herbs. Hardly any companion is more subtly complementary than bronze fennel, *Foeniculum vulgare* 'Purpureum'; both plants reach their zeniths in late summer.

GOLDEN YELLOW

ABUTILON PICTUM 'GOLD DUST' (above) HAS
APRICOT BELL FLOWERS. VARIEGATED BRASSICA
(opposite) BLOOMS IN A BORDER AT GREAT
DIXTER, ENGLAND.

ABUTILON PICTUM

When a leaf is variegated with pure white, that portion has no chlorophyll and could not long survive without its green parts. However, when the variegation is yellow or gold, the color comes from the pigments carotene and xanthophyll.

The type of yellow variegation seen in certain flowering maples, *Abutilon*, is caused by a virus, harmless to the host plant and not transferable to other species or varieties in the same genus. Abutilons of this type first became popular around the turn of the century for bedding-out. They were propagated from tip cuttings and trained both as bushes and tree-form standards.

Abutilon megapotamicum 'Variegata' has gold-mottled leaves and a decumbent habit that suits it to hanging baskets or spilling over the sides of a window box. *Abutilon pictum* 'Gold Dust' grows vigorously, with bright green leaves that are heavily spotted with gold. Orange bell flowers appear nonstop. *Abutilon pictum* 'Thompsonii' is compact and upright, with yellow-mottled leaves and a profusion of luminous orange flowers. There are also abutilons having white-variegated leaves, for a silvery effect. These include 'Clementine Variegated' (white lacings in green leaves; bright red flowers), 'Savitzii' (dwarf, like a variegated Japanese maple, with snow white marblings in green leaves), and 'Souvenir de Bonn' (white marbling in green foliage, large orange flowers).

Abutilons grow rapidly in warm temperatures with a half day or more of sun. In these conditions they can assimilate lots of water and nutrients. The response will be colorful foliage and a profusion of bell-shaped flowers. As houseplants, abutilons flower best if there is at least a 10° difference between day and night temperatures. They are prone to whiteflies, but spraying the undersides of leaves with insecticidal soap once a week will keep them clean.

BRASSICA VARIEGATA

Hardly any gardener sets out to collect only plants having variegated leaves, although it may seem so, to cynics who view this sort of special interest as esoteric to the point of madness. Nonetheless plants with variegated leaves exert a fascination fodils and tulips, creamy and yellow forms of which will play up the creamy yellow in its leaves. In front as edging might be planted any number of self-colored pansies or violas whose flowers are entirely pale yellow to lemony. The type of variega-

which I believe is irresistible to true gardeners. Witness, for instance, the highly yellow-variegated *Brassica*, a cress or mustard, flowering in the herbaceous beds in high spring at Great Dixter in England, where Christopher Lloyd, one of the most famous gardeners of our time, is the master. Variegated brassica grows quickly in the spring and blooms along with the daffodils. tion seen here in the photograph of brassica may or may not be carried in the seeds. A similar-looking variegation, except in creamy white, is seen in the money plant, *Lunaria annua* 'Variegata Stella', seeds of which are offered by Thompson & Morgan (see Resources). Both are Crucifers, so it is feasible that variegated brassica can be grown from seed.

CANNA
'STRIPED BEAUTY'

When certain acid-loving plants turn yellow in response to soil pH that is too alkaline, the main rib and veins remain green, a sign of iron deprivation. If, however, the veins are yellow and the leaf tissue itself is green, as in *Canna* × *generalis* 'Striped Beauty', which was found in Thailand, the plant is healthy and a true variegate. 'Striped Beauty' looks remarkable in any situation but is seen to great advantage when gently back- or side-lighted, early or late in the day. Then the fresh spring green

of the leaves and the golden veins will fairly glow. 'Striped Beauty' requires the same care as plain cannas and can be containerized.

Alpinia zerumbet 'Variegata', the variegated shell ginger, is remarkably similar — at a glance. But when the two are closely compared, it becomes apparent that while in the canna the yellow lines are precisely and evenly spaced, in the ginger they are highly irregular in width. In some variegated plants the color is transient according to the progression of the growing season. In the canna and the ginger it is constant, but in *Iris pseudacorus* 'Variegata' the emerging leaves are strongly striped yellow but by midsummer they turn entirely green.

CHAMAECYPARIS

Conifers are a major source of color in the landscape and not only in summer. Many of the golden forms intensify their color in winter the same as those that are blue or reddish. The golden Hinoki cypress, *Chamaecyparis obtusa* 'Crippsii', is a Japanese native of pyramidal form that grows slowly to eight or 10 feet tall. The brilliant yellow color persists at the foliage tips year-round, in Zones 4 to 8. In another cultivar from this same genus and species, 'Nana Lutea', the golden, fanned foliage is noticeably brighter in late spring and early summer, then turning bronze as autumn temperatures plummet. Siting the plant in full sun or very light shade brings out the gold. Another

CANNA 'STRIPED BEAUTY' (left) STANDS OUT ON THE TERRACE OF NEW YORK CITY GARDENER VICTOR NELSON. *CHAMAECYPARIS* (opposite) IS DISPLAYED IN A CLASSIC CONCRETE URN IN THE PENNSYLVANIA GARDEN OF J. LIDDON PENNOCK, JR.

dwarf golden Hinoki is 'Kamaeni Hiba', which has more thread-like foliage than 'Nana Lutea'. In 'Tetragona Aurea' the irregular golden branch tips point in an upward direction on a plant that can grow six feet tall by three feet wide in a decade.

These or other golden conifers (such as a golden form of dwarf pine, *Pinus densiflora* 'Pendula') can be made to appear even more yellow in winter with nearby plantings of some of the strongly upright vertical branches of yellow-twig dogwood, *Cornus sericea* 'Flaviramea'. Or echo the color with a golden ground cover, such as *Juniperus horizontalis* 'Mother Lode' (which is said to have originated from a plain green plant that was struck by lightning). A red-tinged, bluish conifer can seem all the more lively in the winter landscape in the company of red-osier dogwood, *Cornus sericea*.

ELAEAGNUS

Spotted elaeagnus, *Elaeagnus pungens* 'Maculata', is rare among broadleaved evergreens and may eventually attain a height of 15 feet, but is hardy only in Zones 7 to 9. The large, evergreen leaves are marked with a dark yellow blotch in the center, with a paler yellow irregular banding between this and the green parts. Other varieties that deserve attention are 'Tricolor' (with yellowish and pink-white variegated leaves) and 'Variegata' (yellowish white-margined leaves). These cultivars are widely used as accent plants in warm regions and can withstand shearing when used as a hedge. A close look reveals brown scales on the branchlets, and the silvery appearance of the leaf reverses. Fragrant, silvery flowers open in early autumn, followed by fruit that is red when ripe. Elaeagnus is outstanding for indoor/outdoor culture in cooler climates.

ELAEAGNUS (above) HAS GLOSSY LEAVES THAT MAY BE COLORED WHITE, SILVERY, OR PURE GOLD. THE *EUGENIA SPRENGERI* PLANT SHOWN (below) IS 15 YEARS OLD, IN A FIVE-INCH CLAY POT AT LOGEE'S GREENHOUSES IN CONNECTICUT.

EUGENIA SPRENGERI

One of the most unusual yellow-green, lime, or chartreuse plants I have seen is a relatively aged specimen of *Eugenia sprengeri* in the collection of Logee's Greenhouses in Connecticut. This eugenia has needle-like leaves resembling those of the asparagus-fern, *Asparagus densiflorus* 'Sprengeri', from which came its specific name, *sprengeri*. This plant grows at an extremely slow pace and is a natural for growing in a blue-glazed bonsai pot. A plant formerly classified as *Eugenia*, now assigned to the genus *Myrciaria*, species *myriophylla*, has been described as the "needle eugenia" and may possibly be one and the same as *E. sprengeri*. By either name these evergreens need a moderate to warm greenhouse in winter, with moist air that circulates freely and a loam-based potting soil kept evenly moist in all seasons.

FRAGARIA VESCA

Curiously, the most sought-after strawberry may be valued not for its fruit but for its creamy white variegated leaves. *Fragaria vesca* 'Albo-marginata' produces red berries of the sweet alpine type. Like any strawberry, 'Albo-marginata' needs well-spaded garden loam, preferably with a top-dressing of compost or rotted manure placed on the soil the previous autumn. *Fragaria vesca* 'Alpine Yellow' has plain green leaves on a runnerless plant and produces pale yellow berries that don't attract birds (but humans love their wild sweetness). Another strawberry of unexpected decorative quality is 'Pink Panda', with a profusion of large rose-pink flowers from spring until autumn-frost, and small, edible fruits. Strawberries need constant moisture and nutrients, and a yearly side-dressing of compost in late autumn.

HEDERA HELIX

Cultivars of English ivy, *Hedera helix*, often have creamy or golden variegation. In 'Buttercup' the leaves are almost entirely glowing yellow, while in 'Gold Heart' the elongated leaves have gold centers and green edges. 'Fantasia' has yellow fleckings in a green ground, with pink stems. If a shoot of new growth on one of these cultivars reverts to solid green, remove it immediately, otherwise this part will tend to outgrow and eventually overtake the variegated portions. This can happen also with variegated hollies and euonymus. Where hederas are concerned, combining two separate plants, each having its own root system, can be highly effective, especially when training as a topiary or espalier. A gold- or silver-variegated form should be paired with another of similar size having plain leaves.

AT BARNSLEY HOUSE ROSEMARY VEREY COVERS THE GROUND WITH VARIEGATED-LEAVED STRAWBERRIES (above). SALLY REATH COMBINES *HEDERA HELIX* 'BUTTERCUP' (below) WITH HOSTA HAVING GREEN-EDGED, GOLDEN LEAVES.

HELICHRYSUM PETIOLARE 'LIMELIGHT'

Licorice plant, *Helichrysum petiolare* (also listed as *H. petiolatum*), is a South African species having leaves so felted with tiny white hairs that they appear silver. In the cultivar 'Limelight' the leaves are the color of lime sherbet, and in 'Variegata' both silver and chartreuse. When stroked, all three smell of anise. They are not frost hardy. In the silvery-leaved species *H. angostifolia* the smell of the leaves is precisely that of curry.

PHILODENDRON SCANDENS 'AUREUM'

Golden green is not a color generally associated with philodendron, but that is precisely the appearance of *Philodendron scandens* 'Aureum', or "limeleaf vine." This beauty can be trained wreath-style around a 12-inch wire or grapevine form that has been anchored upright. Provide average house warmth and keep the soil moist.

THE GOLDEN FORM OF DWARF PINE, *PINUS DENSIFLORA* 'PENDULA' (opposite, upper), LOOKS MORE YELLOW IN WINTER. *SOLEIROLIA SOLEIROLII* 'AUREA' (opposite, lower) IS A TINY-LEAVED GROUND COVER.

PINUS

The 'Aurea' form of *Pinus densiflora* 'Pendula' has golden green needles that bring unexpected color to a conifer collection in all seasons, but especially in winter when the effect is heightened. In the variety 'Alboterminata' the tips of the needles are yellowish white. The 'Aurea' variety of Scotch pine, *P. sylvestris*, has needles that are golden yellow until mature. In the 'Oculus-draconis' variety of Japanese black pine, *P. thunbergiana*, the needles have two distinctive yellow bands.

Some other woody plants that could serve to bring out the gold of any of these pines are *Sambucus racemosa* 'Plumosa Aurea', a yellow-leaved shrub; *Spirea japonica* 'Goldflame' (young leaves blend red, copper, and orange, changing to pure gold at midseason and reverting to the combination in autumn); and *Acer japonicum* 'Aureum', the golden full moon maple.

SOLEIROLIA SOLEIROLII 'AUREA'

Golden-leaved baby's-tears, *Soleirolia soleirolii* 'Aurea', is precisely the color of limeleaf vine, *Philodendron scandens* 'Aurea', as if from the same dye lot, yet baby's-tears belongs to the nettles, philodendron to the aroids. Soleirolia, also called *Helxine*, is from the Mediterranean and suffers when temperatures drop below 50°F. An ideal use for it is as ground cover for large container plants. Another application is in the making of moss-stuffed topiaries, such as in alternating bands with the plain green to suggest the stripes of a tiger (seen at the Philadelphia Flower Show). Baby's-tears is one of those plants that can become a weed or can rot or dry off and refuse to grow. Relatively high light produces the best coloring.

CHAPTER
EIGHT

THE
INDOOR
GARDEN

Some of the most adventurous gardeners are those who grow plants indoors all year, or who because of climatic restrictions keep container plants indoors in cold weather, and outdoors in the warm seasons. Sunny windows are a help to indoor gardeners but much can be accomplished in a fluorescent-light garden that has at least four 40-watt bulbs (half of which are warm white and half cool white) placed in one or more shop light reflectors. Suspend the lights 18 to 24 inches above a plant bench or table measuring four feet long by up to two feet wide, and have the lights turned on for 16 hours out of every 24. ❧ One compelling reason to grow plants indoors is that they give the gardener something to do during the seasons, kinds of weather, or times of day that discourage outdoor activities. Gardening indoors also allows gardeners to help preserve plants' genetic diversity. There are undoubtedly numerous plants being cultivated in private gardens that are extinct or nearly so in their native habitats. Tropical rainforest species, in particular, are rapidly disappearing in the wild, but can often be accommodated indoors in conditions familiar to them. Such plants are right at home in the sorts of indoor gardens where gesneriads and begonias, aroids, orchids, and bromeliads are already being grown successfully. ❧ Indoor gardeners can also help preserve desert or dryland species, a task that is often best accomplished by harvesting from the natural habitat only the seeds, so that the population of any given species can be increased without risk to the source. The preservation of genetic diversity hardly needs defending, but an excellent example of why exploration and cultivation of new plants must continue can be seen in Kalanchoe farinosa, a beautiful succulent that flowers during the long days of the year instead of the short, which is the habit of the kalanchoes currently sold as seasonal flowering pot plants. Kalanchoe farinosa is a lovely plant in and of itself, but its ability to flower regardless of the day length lends commercial value as well. Another avenue of adventure indoors is to explore the world of miniatures. There are tiny species and cultivars of a wide variety of plants, including orchids, roses, African violets, florist gloxinia, and other species of Sinningia, begonias, philodendrons, caladiums, ferns, and a host of others. ❧ The indoor gardener's greatest source of material is a willing and active imagination, the derring-do to simply take a plant that is attractive or appealing, put it in a pot, and have a go with it as a houseplant. It also helps to break the sill habit — that misguided notion that indoor plants must be pressed against the windows in order to grow properly. If they are set on the floor or else on shelves a few feet back from a sunny exposure, for example, the gardener can walk between them and the window wall, and thus be better able to appreciate the plants and to supply their needs.

ANISODONTEA CAPENSIS (preceding two pages) IS A MINIATURE
CHINESE HIBISCUS. *LENOPHYLLUM LINGUA* (opposite) HAS COLONIZED
IN THE PHILADELPHIA COLLECTION OF ERNESTA BALLARD.

ABUTILON

The genus *Abutilon* is comprised of well over a hundred different species, from most tropical and warm-temperate regions of the world. Best known are those cultivated as houseplants, or grown outdoors in warm weather, such as the flowering maples, so called for the shape of the leaves. A natural hybrid between *A. megapotamicum* and *A. pictum*, *A. × milleri*, and cultivars of it, are often seen as wall shrubs in England and the Pacific Northwest. C. Z. Guest trains *A. × milleri* as a potted living wreath, using a 10-inch azalea pot and an 18-inch wire wreath form, anchored upright with stakes. In any garden setting the crimson-veined, apricot-yellow bell flowers have a charm all their own. There are also the abutilons that have variegated leaves (see Chapter Seven). One of the best cultivars is 'Moonchimes', which is naturally dwarf and also sterile, so that the unusually large and luminous yellow flowers appear in unbelievable numbers for a seemingly endless season. It is readily trainable as a hanging plant or tree-form standard, which can be from three to five feet tall, depending on the situation.

Besides proffering the hollyhock-like bell flowers associated with romantic cottage gardens, abutilons can also be nearly everblooming. They need sun, warmth, fresh, moist air circulation, and an all-purpose potting mix that is well-drained, adequately watered, and regularly fertilized. When abutilons are outdoors in warm weather, they almost invariably bloom freely. Indoors they may balk if night temperatures are not at least ten degrees cooler on average than those by day. Keep inevitable whiteflies in check with insecticidal soap.

DOUBLE-FLOWERED ACHIMENES (above right) WAS DEVELOPED UNDER THE THIRD GENERATION OF THE PARK FAMILY TO WORK WITH THIS SUMMER-FLOWERING GESNERIAD.

ACHIMENES

Achimenes is a gesneriad that grows from scaly rhizomes planted in spring an inch deep, an inch or so apart, six to an eight-inch pot or basket, in a warm, bright place. The stems may be upright or trailing, with opposite or whorled leaves an inch or two long, from pale green to reddish bronze. The tubular, five-lobed or semidouble hose-in-hose flowers appear all summer until the nights become chilly in autumn. Colors include blue, crimson, lavender, pink, purple, scarlet, violet, white, and

yellow, often with splashes or veining in a contrasting hue.

Achimenes were so popular with the Victorians that they gave them all sorts of names — Japanese pansy, hot water plant, kimono plant, nut orchid, widow's tears, cupid's bower, magic flower — and also formally named every new seedling whose flowers showed the slightest variation from existing varieties. They were possibly as widely cultivated a hundred years ago as the then unknown but related African violet, *Saintpaulia*, is today. Lately breeders have been working again on the achimenes, making them all the more worth growing in a mostly shaded summer garden.

ACORUS

Acorus gramineus, a foot-tall Japanese aroid that has grass-like foliage, 'Pusillus' (a three-inch miniature), and a miniature sweet flag, *Acorus calamus*, along with its cultivars 'Variegatus' (with cream-striped leaves) are among the bog or aquatic plants that can be grown in containers. While winter-hardy to Zone 5 or below 0°F., they are also adaptable to growing indoors all year, or outdoors when the weather is reasonably warm and settled. In addition to the cultivars mentioned above, Glasshouse Works Greenhouses lists 'Dwarf Himemasamune' (interlacing ranks of sword-shaped, glossy, white-striped green leaves in four-inch cushions), 'Masamune' (white-striped leaves, similar to 'Variegatus' but more compact), 'Minimus Aureus' (tiny, flat, bright chartreuse leaves in tufts), 'Oborozuki' (evergreen with a golden grass effect, six-inch ranks of leaves; suggested for a blue bonsai pot), 'Tanimanoyuki' (yellow-striped, slim blades), and 'Yodonoyuki' (a very rare Japanese selection of the grassy-leaved sweet flag with overlapping six-inch leaves banded in creamy ochre).

Also suited to culture as indoor/outdoor boggy or aquatic containerized plants are innumerable sedges — species from the genera *Cyperus*, *Carex*, and *Juncus* — that may be purchased by name, or in some instances may be dug from one's own property with or without specific identification. There are also other aroids besides *Acorus*, such as *Colocasia esculenta* 'Fontanesia', described by Glasshouse Works as having "vigorous, purple-stemmed elephant-eared leaves of glaucous blue-green." The plant needs warmth and constantly moist soil to thrive.

AQUATIC PLANTS *ACORUS*, *COLOCASIA*, AND A REED-LIKE SEDGE GROW IN A TANK (right), IN THE STEINHARDT CONSERVATORY AT BROOKLYN BOTANIC GARDEN.

AMORPHOPHALLUS

Amorphophallus rivieri is one of the more curious plants that gardeners choose to cultivate, as its names indicate. The plant is called devil's-tongue (for the fetid, liver-purple spathe), leopard palm (for the purple-spotted, brownish green, stalk-like petiole to three or four feet tall), and umbrella arum (a more scientifically based name, referring to the much-divided and solitary leaf blade that spreads umbrella-like to four feet across). Its tu-

bers can grow up to a foot in diameter. 'Konjac', a cultivar, is the voodoo-lily of commerce, promoted and grown as a curiosity in the West but planted from Indonesia to Japan for the edible corms. Both plants can be grown indoors if there is no place for them outdoors in summer: Let the soil dry in autumn, at which time the leaf will disappear.

Amorphophallus titanum, the Titan arum, from Sumatra, is similar but not a choice for indoor gardeners. This monster has leaves up to 15 feet wide, and an unpleasant-smelling six-foot spadix (flower spike). This structure holds claim to being one of the largest inflorescences among known herbaceous plants.

ANISODONTEA

Anisodontea capensis, also known as *A.* × *hypomandarum* or as a member of the related genus, *Malvastrum*, is a South African member of the Mallow Family. From spring to autumn it has five-petaled, bowl-shaped blossoms to an inch or so across, rose-magenta with darker veins radiating from the center; the plant will also produce some flowers through the winter if it is given a warm, sunny, moist location. Anisodontea resembles a miniature Chinese hibiscus, growing to three feet tall and nearly as wide. It has been cherished as an evergreen shrublet in the mildest English gardens for some time, but is newly cultivated in the United States. Breeders hope to bring out other colors and larger flowers.

BLOODFLOWER, *ASCLEPIAS CURASSAVICA*, IS A SUBTROPICAL MILKWEED THAT BLOOMS MOSTLY IN SUMMER AND FALL. IT CAN BE AN ANNUAL OR PERENNIAL, DEPENDING ON THE CLIMATE.

The plant is frost-tender but in winter can be kept on the dry side in any sun-heated pit or sun porch where temperatures stay above freezing. The plants will grow from seeds planted where there is constant warmth in the spring, or from cuttings of new to half-mature wood in late summer or early autumn. When newly rooted and small enough, the cuttings make nice flowering plants for a fluorescent-light garden. Grow this little mallow as a bush, in a pot, or set into the ground of a cottage garden in warm weather; or train it as a tree-form standard to four or five feet, a process that can be accomplished in two seasons. Thereafter the head can be cut back by two-thirds in late winter or spring, in order to maintain the desired size. Root pruning and repotting at the same time will assure a vital plant that can be kept for many years.

ASCLEPIAS CURASSAVICA

Asclepias curassavica is a subtropical milkweed growing to three or four feet tall, with narrow, glossy leaves, to seven inches long, set close around the stem. The reddish purple flowers are capped by yellow-orange hoods. Also called bloodflower, this species is one of the plants featured at the Day Butterfly Center at Callaway Gardens in Georgia. The precise origins of *curassavica* are unknown, but it is probably from South America. The plant is described as a perennial hardy to Zone 7, or suited to treatment as an annual. It is actually a tuberous, ev-

CALIFORNIA GARDENER MABEL CORWIN SHOWS OFF 'CHRISTMAS CANDY', THE CULTIVAR SHE BRED BY MATING AN UNIDENTIFIED SPECIES WITH *B. × SEMPERFLORENS* 'GLAMOUR ROSE PICOTEE'.

ergreen, bushy sub-shrub suited to year-round culture outdoors in the United States only in the warmest climates.

Since the primary flowering season is summer to autumn, bloodflower makes an ideal indoor-outdoor container plant, easily started from seeds in a warm, sunny window or light garden for bloom later in the same season. The choice plants can be held over in a cool but frost-free place and kept on the dry side, until the beginning of the next outdoor growing cycle. If a potted specimen of *curassavica* is held in such conditions over autumn and early winter, then cut back and placed in a warm, moist, sunny atmosphere such as a greenhouse or sunporch, it can be brought to bloom in the spring and will continue flowering until autumn. The catalogue of J. L. Hudson, *Seedsman*, of Redwood City, California, says that *A. curassavica* hosts the monarch, and the fiber from its stems has been spun and the seed floss used in pillows.

BEGONIA

Amateur begonia grower Mabel Corwin changed the way the world looks at the wax begonia, *Begonia × semperflorens*, when in the 1980s she crossed an unidentified species grown from seeds obtained through the American Begonia Society's Seed Fund with the bedding-plant hybrid 'Glamour Rose Picotee'. The result, which she christened 'Christmas Candy', was a taller, larger-leaved, more graceful plant than the commercial wax

begonia, with large, outward-reaching cymes of glowing orange-red flowers in extraordinary profusion. Propagation must be by duplicating the original cross and growing from seeds.

Other breeders have followed Corwin's example, some results of their efforts being 'Amigo Pink' (individual salmon-pink flowers to over two inches across, with glossy, angel-wing leaves and a trailing habit ideal for hanging basket culture) and 'Pink Avalanche Hybrid' (sterile, which means the plant produces no seeds but tremendous numbers of its pink, one-inch flowers). The new *B. × semperflorens* hybrids can be grown in summer gardens or as houseplants.

BRASSAVOLA

Brassavola is a tropical American genus of some 15 different epiphytic orchids with stem-like pseudobulbs. They are allied with Cattleya and certain of them, particularly *B. digbyana* and *B. nodosa* (lady-of-the-night), were among the first orchids to be promoted as houseplants. In addition, *B. digbyana* figures in the parentage of hybrids involving *Cattleya*, *Laelia*, and *Sophronitis*, in particular those with prominent, fringed lips. At

Lauray of Salisbury, in Connecticut, I first became aware of *B. perrinii* by its scent; then I noticed its distinctive flowers.

Originally from Brazil and Paraguay, brassavola thrives on summer warmth, high light intensities, and fairly constant high humidity. Cooler and drier conditions in winter, followed by spring's increasing warmth and moisture bring on summer bloom. These plants are naturals for hanging outdoors in summer, from a tree or in a slathouse, and some will no doubt provide a surprising bonus of autumn and winter blooms.

BRUGMANSIA

There are two types of blossoms known as angel trumpets: those that point outward belong to *Datura*, and those that dangle to *Brugmansia*. Brugmansias are usually treated as tender perennial shrubs and daturas as annuals, although not every datura is, strictly speaking, a plant that completes its entire life cycle from seed to seed in a single season. At the risk of making another generalization, brugmansias are more likely than daturas to adapt, as container plants, to an indoor-outdoor existence. There is a classic woodcut from the nineteenth century that shows a dangling angel trumpet trained as a tree-form standard to about six feet tall, with an idealized placement of uniformly perfect leaves circling at the upper levels and beneath them an unbelievable profusion of perfect, evenly spaced blossoms. C. Z. Guest has shown in her gardens in Old Westbury, Long Island, that the woodcut may not have been as much exaggerated as might previously have been thought, especially when the brugmansia is 'Jamaica Yellow' or 'Charles Grimaldi', a California hybrid with 15-inch yellow-orange flowers and strongly recurved petal tips.

'Charles Grimaldi' flowers grow well all year in warm temperatures and high light, with adequate water and nutrients, and give off a wonderful scent. A tree-size specimen needs at least a 15-inch tub, a whiskey barrel being ideal to support a show of one hundred or more blossoms at once. Shrub-size brugmansias can be accommodated in smaller pots.

Other cultivars include 'Betty Marshall' (many single white flowers with a spicy sweet scent, on compact plants), *B.* × *candida* 'Double White' (the only double-flowered brugmansia), *B.* × *insignis* 'Frosty Pink' (salmon-pink flowers turning darker as they age), *B. sanguinea* 'Inca Queen' (yellow-veined orange-red trumpets; requires cool conditions), and *B. versicolor* (white flowers that age to apricot-peach).

GARDENING COLUMNIST C. Z. GUEST ADMIRES
THE GOLDEN-TRUMPET BRUGMANSIA SHE HAS
TRAINED INTO A TREE-FORM STANDARD.

BRUNFELSIA

Yesterday-today-and-tomorrow describes the fragrant blossoms of *Brunfelsia*, a South American tomato relative with blossoms that change color daily, fading from an intense periwinkle blue to near white, or, in some species, from white to cream or pale yellow. The plant itself can be a handsome glossy leaved shrub, grown outdoors in Zone 10, or Zone 9 if protected. Gardeners elsewhere can grow it in a pot as an indoor/outdoor subject.

The blue-violet flowers of *B. australis* open from early spring to autumn. It often appears as an award-winning container shrub at the Philadelphia Flower Show in early March, to three or four feet tall and almost completely covered with the white-eyed blue-violet flowers in various stages and hues. Another species, *B. pauciflora* 'Macrantha', is blue-purple and larger, the individual blossoms to more than two inches across. *B. jamaicensis*, a currently endangered species from the Blue Mountains of Jamaica, has long, tubular white-to-cream flowers that scent the evening air from early spring to autumn. Fortunately this species is being propagated commercially and cultivated increasingly even as it disappears from the wild.

If the brunfelsias have a drawback it is that their great beauty causes gardeners to assume, when they first encounter the plant, that it must demand special care and growing conditions that are difficult to provide. But such is not the case. Small specimens kept somewhat rootbound in a five-inch pot can bloom intermittently indoors for months on end in a sunny, warm, moist situation. Brunfelsias respond well to a humusy, loam-based formula such as equal parts of garden loam, peat moss, clean sand, and well-rotted compost or leaf mold. The addition of a handful of dried cow manure to each quart of potting mix boosts growth following a late winter or early spring repotting. The plants also need regular applications of fertilizer. Brunfelsias are surprisingly insect-free.

CRASSULA

There are in South Africa about three hundred different species of *Crassula*, a member of the Orpine Family, which includes in addition some of the world's favorite plants: *Adromischus*, *Aeonium*, *Echeveria*, *Kalanchoe*, *Sedum*, and *Sempervivum*, to name a few. To grow or know only the jade plant, *C. argentea*, is to miss out on some of the most interesting succulents that can be cultivated. In fact, you needn't look beyond the varieties and cultivars of the species itself to find some fas-

cinating and very different plants. *Crassula argentea* 'Sunset', for example, has glowing golden leaves that are edged in red. In 'Gollum' the bright green leaves are rolled together, appearing open at the tips. Full sun, fresh air circulation, and temperatures above freezing are the basic conditions crassulas need, along with a well-drained, gritty potting mix. One of the most unusual is the "moss" crassula, *C. lycopodioides*, its stems completely covered by scale-like leaves in four ranks, giving a squared appearance.

CURCUMA

Curcuma and two allied genera from the Ginger Family, Globba and Kaempferia, include tuberous-rooted species that often die to the ground during a season of rest (winter), during which time they can be kept nearly dry in a dark place where temperatures are moderate, such as a cupboard or closet. Curcuma roscoeana is one of the most unusual, an Indian species that was thought to be extinct until it was discovered growing in a Florida collector's garden in the 1960s. The oblong leaves, to a foot long, grow on a stem to two or three feet tall, from the center of which arises the inflorescence, a torch of long-lasting

CRASSULA ARGENTEA 'GOLLUM' (opposite, far left upper) HAS ROLLED OR FLUTED LEAVES. CURCUMA ROSCOEANA (opposite, far left lower) HAS A LONG-LASTING BRACT, TOWARD THE TOP OF WHICH ARE BORNE RELATIVELY SHORT-LIVED YELLOW TRUE BLOSSOMS. ELEPHANT'S-FOOT DESCRIBES THE CAUDEX FORMED BY SPECIES OF DIOSCOREA SUCH AS D. MACROSTACHYS (opposite, near left).

orange bracts, the upper ones revealing briefly the small yellow true flowers.

Globba winitii, from Thailand, grows to 18 inches tall, forming a clump of many light green leaves that in early autumn is much decorated by nearly indescribable waxy, yellow-orange "dancing lady" blossoms from purple-violet bracts. Kaempferia pulchra (from Thailand and the Malay Archipelago) and peacock lily, K. roscoeana (from Burma), have stemless leaves at ground level that are delicately variegated in the subtle manner of changeable satin. From the base are borne violet-like flowers that last one day each, on plants of a size easily managed along with African violets in a window or light garden.

DIOSCOREA

Caudex-forming plants have been around no doubt for some millions of years, but only now are they becoming popular for house and container gardens. Also called caudiciform, such plants occur in several families. All these plants form enlarged stems, a means of storing water against periods of drought.

Dioscorea macrostachya might be mistaken for an ordinary morning-glory vine, but if one traces the stem to the base, one finds something resembling an elephant's foot, albeit a vegetable one. The plant is also known as D. elephantipes. It belongs to the Yam Family, source of the vitamin A-rich tubers that in D. batatas and other species are an important food crop around the world. The species cultivated as ornamentals need a porous medium in a shallow pot, so that there is no place for water to be trapped. These plants like it sunny and hot in spring and summer, then go dormant in autumn.

Another genus with caudex-forming species is Dorstenia, a member of the Fig or Mulberry Family, with an inflorescence something like an inside-out fig, from which small seeds are shot out some distance from the parent when they are ripe.

One of the most familiar caudiciforms is the ponytail palm or elephant-foot tree, Beaucarnea recurvata, a member of the Agave Family from Mexico, that is now propagated from seeds and marketed the world over as a popular houseplant. Another is Adenium obesum, a name that sort of says it all. A member of the Dogbane Family, it is known as desert rose, for the large pink to red flowers that appear at the beginning of active growth, in late winter to early spring.

Hydnophytum formicarum maintains a symbiotic relationship with certain ants who use its tunneled and cavernous above-ground caudex as something of an apartment house, in the process also assisting in the plant's pollination and in providing nutrients to the roots.

FUCHSIA

There are summer garden fuchsias, hardy fuchsias, and then there is the honeysuckle fuchsia, so-called because its dangling flowers resemble coral or trumpet honeysuckle, *Lonicera semper-virens*. Besides an attractive, upright bushy habit and satiny, purplish olive leaves, the special beauty of *Fuchsia triphylla* 'Gartenmeister Bohnstedt' lies in its ability to flower all year in much warmer conditions than the others; it will bloom in

sunny winter windows, light gardens, and home greenhouses.

Honeysuckle fuchsia's behavior is explained by its descent from a West Indian species observed originally in Haiti and Santo Domingo. The temperatures, air quality, and day length in that part of the world can be readily approximated indoors in northern gardens. 'Gartenmeister Bohnstedt', a 1905 German introduction, keeps blooming but will need summer shade in the hottest climates. It can be grown as a bush, to two or three feet, in a hanging basket or trained as a tree-form standard. Alas, like other fuchsias, this gets whiteflies.

HOYA

When gardeners hear *Hoya* they immediately think of a vine, but *Hoya multiflora* (also known as *Centrostoma multiflora*) has an upright and shrubby habit. For being nearly everblooming, *H. multiflora* was called to my attention by veteran plantsman and global plant hunter Jean Merkel, whose establishment Alberts & Merkel Brothers, Inc., in Florida, has been for generations the source of untold treasures in the form of orchids, aroids, and other plants of tropical rain forests. While the habit of this species is different from the common hoyas, it does have typically waxy leaves and white flowers in the clusters one expects of a member of the Milkweed Family. In *H. multiflora* the

THIS HONEYSUCKLE FUCHSIA (left), THE CULTIVAR 'GARTENMEISTER BOHNSTEDT', GRACES SALLY REATH'S PENNSYLVANIA TERRACE. *HOYA MULTIFLORA* (opposite) BLOOMS CONSTANTLY FOR FLORIDA GROWER JEAN MERKEL.

reflexed individual blossoms give an appearance of openness or outward thrust from the center, like fireworks going off.

Glasshouse Works Greenhouses in Ohio, is the source of another shrubby species, *H. odorata* (or *H. eugeniafolia*), with thin, upright, arching stems, bronzy new leaves, and small umbels of pink and tan-rose flowers in winter along the semi-deciduous stems. Also of note is *H. pubera*, a bushlet of pelted small leaves with many clusters of about a dozen pink, faintly scented flowers with bright pink centers, usually in late summer and early autumn.

As houseplants these hoyas need constant warmth, an abundance of sun or fluorescent light, and high humidity. If they can be placed outdoors in warm weather, so much the better.

SINNINGIA

Sinningia is the Brazilian gesneriad that gives us not only the popular commercial florist gloxinia but a host of other species and hybrids, from plants smaller than a teacup to specimens as big around as a bushel basket. Some of the most spectacular florist gloxinias ever cultivated have come from the breeding efforts of Connecticut grower Albert Buell, who was a machinist at the time he first dabbled some pollen among the standard Belgian Hybrids that were growing in his bay window garden. Beginning with the introduction of the first Buell Hybrids in 1949, Buell became a full-time grower and breeder, who was eventually to specialize in African violets and other gesneriads. Some of his most exquisite sinningia blossoms, in both trumpet and slipper shapes, single and double, are those having a white ground which is finely speckled with pink, rose, or carmine.

BUELL HYBRID GLOXINIAS OF THE FLORIST TYPE ARE NOTEWORTHY FOR THE DOTTED-SWISS EFFECT SEEN IN THIS SEMIDOUBLE.

While growers go to extraordinary lengths to be able to grow this kind of gloxinia in fluorescent-light gardens, with blooms all year-round, Buell uses appropriately shaded and ventilated greenhouses and follows one growth cycle yearly, planting seeds in late autumn or winter, or bulbs in spring, for summer flowers. After blooming, the plants go through a gradual drying off until the tubers go dormant in autumn. In winter the tubers are stored in a dark place at 58° to 60°F. To duplicate this cycle at home, use a protected porch for the main summer growth and flowering. Another species, *S. canescens* (formerly *Rechsteineria leucotricha* and *Gesneria cardinalis*), is called Brazilian edelweiss, for the silver-pelted leaves. The slim, tubular red flowers (white in 'Innocence') are densely haired.

STREPTOSOLEN

Orange browallia, *Streptosolen jamesonii*, a plant from Columbia and Ecuador named for the shape of its flowers, which resemble those of a related plant in the Nightshade Family, adopts a sprawling posture, somewhere between a shrub and a climber. In Zone 10 (9 with protection) it is a splendid plant to train as a wall shrub. Elsewhere orange browallia is grown as a greenhouse or sun porch plant for winter and spring bloom, with intermediate temperatures of 50° to 70°F. It can also be used as a hanging plant or trained in standard form for bedding out in summer; a standard can be wintered over in a frost-free place such as a sun-heated pit. Propagate new plants from cuttings of last year's wood. Water freely when in active growth; maintain drier during an annual rest, then prune and repot.

TREVESIA

Trevesia palmata of the Aralia Family is a small evergreen tree to 20 feet, native from northern India to southwestern China. Its intricately cut and palmately lobed leaves, to two feet across, have a sort of duck-foot webbing extending outward from the center or sinus area of the leaf that is perhaps unique in the plant world. Trevesia can be grown outdoors in tropical and subtropical gardens. Elsewhere it makes an unusual houseplant for any environment where such related plants as aralia, dizygotheca, hedera, polyscias, and schefflera will thrive. Give trevesia filtered sun, fresh, moist air, and moderate to warm temperatures.

Snowflake plant, *T. p.* 'Micholitzii', is a cultivar that has silvery white variegation in its glossy green leaves. Mature trevesias bear panicles of creamy white flowers. In cultivation the surest means of propagation is air-layering.

ORANGE BROWALLIA (above) IS *STREPTOSOLEN JAMESONII*, SEEN BLOOMING IN SPRING IN A GREENHOUSE AT LOGEE'S IN CONNECTICUT. *TREVESIA PALMATA* (below) IS AN ENGLISH IVY RELATIVE HAVING UNIQUELY CUT LEAVES.

VIOLA

Two members of the genus *Viola* are of special interest to gardeners who enjoy container culture. *Viola hederacea*, ivy-leaved or Tasmanian violet, is from Australia. It is a stemless, tufted, stolon-producing plant to let spill from a hanging basket or over the side of a window box. Tasmanian violet can also be grown as ground cover for the soil surface around container trees. The small flowers are nearly everblooming, bluish to violet-purple, white-tipped and, according to Logee's catalogue, ". . . accented with a little bird-like orange 'beak'." The plant is evergreen and does best when not subjected to temperatures below 28°F.

The other *Viola* is represented by the fragrant and Parma violets that have been important in perfumery since the 1700s. Logee's catalogue explains that sweet-scented violets were an emblem for Napoleon Bonaparte, and nosegays of the fragrant flowers were worn during the eighteenth and nineteenth centuries. Parma violets can be planted in gardens as far north as Zone 6, and the other fragrant violets are hardy to Zone 4. They are also perfect to keep over winter in a cold greenhouse, so that the flowers that come out in response to warm spells can be properly appreciated. 'Duchess de Parme', introduced in 1870, is a fully double Parma violet, with flowers of intense lavender blue. 'Marie Louise', named for Napoleon's second wife, is also double, a dark lavender. 'Swanley White', from 1883, is a fully double Parma, white with a tint of blue. *Viola odorata* is the dark blue fragrant violet; 'Rosea' is pink and the best all-year bloomer. 'Prince of Wales', from 1889, was once the most popular large-flowered fragrant blue violet.

VIOLA HEDERACEA IS A TUFTED AND
STOLONIFEROUS AUSTRALIAN SPECIES THAT
MAKES A PERFECT HANGING PLANT.

ZYGOPETALUM

Alphabetically speaking, one might think this the last genus of orchids but it is probably the penultimate, preceding as it does *Zygosepalum*. The genera are in fact allied, *Zygosepalum labiosum* having previously been called *Zygopetalum rostratum*. The zygopetalums are epiphytes, native to Central and South America, with egg-shaped pseudobulbs and pleated lance-shaped leaves. The flower racemes, from 18 to 30 inches long, typically have five or six blossoms that are not only showy, but often combine unaccustomed shades of purple, brown, and green. In *Z. mackayi* the yellowish green flower is spotted with brownish purple, the large, spread white lip striped with blue-purple. The flowers, each up to three inches across, are delightfully fragrant and bloom in winter or spring. In the variety 'Crinitum' the greenish flowers are spotted with brown, and the hairy white lip is streaked with violet-blue.

These orchids do nicely in medium-sized fir-bark chips, with about a half cup of horticultural charcoal chips mixed into each quart (or each five-inch pot). Be sure to repot before the old medium starts to decompose. In regard to watering, like epiphytes in general, the zygopetalums (and zygosepalum) need a drench-and-dry cycle with no lingering at either extreme. Obviously, more water and liquid fertilizer are needed in warm, sunny weather, less water (and no fertilizer) in cool or cloudy times. And in the yearly scheme, a winter of intermediate temperatures in a sunny window or greenhouse, with moist air but definitely on the dry side at the roots, followed by a spring and summer of abundant warmth, moisture, and nutrients, leads to the generous annual flowering. These brief guidelines serve the needs of a vast number of orchids — including species such as the *Vanda* and the *Vandopsis* (overleaf) — that beckon every gardener in whose veins there runs the slightest longing for adventure.

SOURCES

VANDA AND *VANDOPSIS* ORCHIDS, HERE BLOOMING
ON A SUNNY TERRACE IN A PALM BEACH GARDEN,
NEED LOTS OF DIRECT SUN IN SPRING AND
SUMMER, IDEALLY OUTDOORS. THEY CAN BE
COOLER AND DRIER AT OTHER TIMES, BUT
ALWAYS NEED FRESH, MOIST CIRCULATING AIR.

Resources

ADAMS COUNTY NURSERY
Box 108
Aspers, PA 17304
Rare apples

ANTIQUE ROSE EMPORIUM
Rt. 5, Box 143
Brenham, TX 77833
Catalogue $2
Old roses, also perennials, ornamental
grasses

APPALACHIAN GARDENS
Box 82
Waynesboro PA 17268
Uncommon woodies

BALDSIEFEN, WARREN
Box 88
Bellvale, NY 10912
Catalogue $3
Azaleas and other rhododendrons

BARNES, VERNON, & SON
Box 250
McMinnville, TN 37110
Uncommon woodies

BEAVER CREEK NURSERY
Box 18243
Knoxville, TN 37928
Catalogue $1
Uncommon woodies

BENJAMIN'S RHODODENDRONS
Box 147
Sumner, WA 98390
Catalogue $3
Azaleas and other rhododendrons

BIOQUEST INTERNATIONAL
Box 5752
Santa Barbara, CA 93150
Catalogue $1
Lachenalias, other bulbs

BLUEMEL, KURT
2740 Greene Lane
Baldwin, MD 21013
Catalogue $2
Ornamental grasses, perennials

BLUESTONE PERENNIALS
7211 Middle Ridge
Madison, OH 44057
Perennials

BORBOLETA GARDENS
15980 Canby Ave., Rt. 5
Faribault, MN 55021
Catalogue $3
Bulbs, tubers, corms, rhizomes

BOVEES NURSERY
1737 S.W. Coronado
Portland, OR 97219
Catalogue $2
Uncommon woodies

BRIARWOOD GARDENS
14 Gully Lane, R.F.D. 1
East Sandwich, MA 02537
List $1
Azaleas and other rhododendrons

BURPEE, W. ATLEE CO.
300 Park Ave.
Warminster, PA 18974
Something for everyone, not necessarily
rare — or common

BUSSE GARDENS
635 E. 7 St.
Cokato, MN 55321
Catalogue $2
Perennials

CAMELLIA FOREST NURSERY
125 Carolina Forest
Chapel Hill, NC 27514
List $1
Uncommon woodies

CANYON CREEK NURSERY
3527 Dry Creek Rd.
Oroville, CA 95965
Silver-leaved plants, plants for Xeriscaping

CARDINAL NURSERY
Rt. 1, Box 316
State Road, NC 28676
Azaleas and other rhododendrons

CARLSON'S GARDENS
Box 305
South Salem, NY 10590
Catalogue $2
Azaleas and other rhododendrons

CARROLL GARDENS
Box 310
Westminster, MD 21157
Catalogue $2
Perennials, woodies, herbs

CATNIP ACRES FARM
67 Christian St.
Oxford, CT 06483
Catalogue $2
Herbs

COASTAL GARDENS
Rt. 3, Box 40
Myrtle Beach, SC 29577
Perennials

COENOSIUM GARDENS
6642 S. Lone Elder Rd.
Aurora, OR 97002
Catalogue $3
Conifers

COLVOS CREEK NURSERY
1931 Second Ave.
Seattle, WA 98101
Catalogue $2
Uncommon woodies

COOK'S GARDEN, THE
Box 65
Londonderry, VT 05148
The best of the best edibles, hybrid and
nonhybrid, domestic and nondomestic

COUNTRY GARDEN, THE
Box 3539
Oakland, CA 94609
Catalogue $2
Outstanding source for seeds of plants,
annual, perennial, biennial, to grow for
cut flowers, fresh and dried; also orna-
mental and heritage wheats

CUMMINS GARDEN, THE
22 Robertsville Rd.
Marlboro, NJ 07746
Catalogue $1
Rhododendrons, azaleas, other woodies

CURTIS, PHILLIP, FARMS
P.O. Box 640
Canby, OR 97013
Woodies and herbaceous plants of note

DAFFODIL MART, THE
Rt. 3, Box 794
Gloucester, VA 23061
List $1
Specialists in *Narcissus* of all kinds; other
bulbs

DODD'S, TOM, RARE PLANTS
Drawer 95
Semmes, AL 36575
List $1
Trees, shrubs, extremely select

DOGWOOD HILLS NURSERY
Rt. 3, Box 181
Franklinton, LA 70438
Catalogue $2
Uncommon plants

EASTERN PLANT SPECIALTIES
Box 226
Georgetown, ME 04548
Catalogue $2
Uncommon woodies, conifers

EDIBLE LANDSCAPING NURSERY
Box 77
Afton, VA 22920

FANCY FRONDS
1911 4th Ave. W.
Seattle, WA 98119
List $1
Ferns

FAR NORTH GARDENS
16785 Harrison Rd.
Livonia, MI 48154
Catalogue $2
Rare primulas, other perennials

FLORA LAN NURSERY
Rt. 1, Box 357
Forest Grove, OR 97116
Uncommon woodies

FOLIAGE GARDENS
2003 128th Ave. S.E.
Bellevue, WA 98005
List $1
Ferns

FOREST FARM
990 Tetherow Rd.
Williams, OR 97544-9599
Catalogue $3
Fascinating woody plants in small sizes
(and affordable prices)

FOXBOROUGH NURSERY
3711 Miller Rd.
Street, MD 21154
List $1
Conifers

FOX HILL FARM
Box 7
Parma, MI 49269
Catalogue $1
Herbs, including about twenty different
basils

FRAGRANT PATH, THE
Box 328
Fort Calhoun, NE 68023
List $1
Fragrant perennials

FRENCH, HOWARD B.
Route 100
Pittsfield, VT 05762
Bulbs

GARDENS OF THE BLUE RIDGE
Box 10
Pineola, NC 28662
Catalogue $2
Wildflowers and ferns

GATHERING GARDEN, THE
Rt. 1, Box 41E
Efland, NC 27243
Perennials

GEORGE, D.S., NURSERIES
2491 Penfield
Fairport, NY 14450
List 50 cents
Clematis

GESNERIAD RESEARCH FOUNDATION
1873 Oak St.
Sarasota, FL 34236
For modest membership fee, members are
able to obtain rare and unusual species

GIRARD NURSERIES
Box 428
Geneva, OH 44041
Uncommon woodies

GLASSHOUSE WORKS GREENHOUSES
Church St.
P.O. Box 97
Stewart, OH 45778-0097
Catalogue $5
Leading collection of plants for container
gardening, indoors and out

GOSSLER FARMS NURSERY
1200 Weaver Rd.
Springfield, OR 97477
List $1
Uncommon woodies

GRAHAM, RUSSELL
4030 Eagle Crest Rd. N.W.
Salem, OR 97304
Catalogue $2
Bulbs, tubers, corms, rhizomes

GREENLADY GARDENS
1415 Eucalyptus Dr.
San Francisco, CA 94132
Catalogue $3
Lachenalias, other bulbs

GREER GARDENS
1280 Goodpasture Island Rd.
Eugene, OR 97401
Catalogue $3
Uncommon woodies, especially
Rhododendron

GRIGSBY CACTUS GARDENS
2326 Bella Vista Dr.
Vista, CA 92084
Catalogue $3
Wide variety of cacti and other succulents, all seed-propagated, not plants
collected from native habitat

GROWERS SERVICE CO.
Box 375
Farmington, MI 48332
List $1
Bulbs, tubers, corms, rhizomes

HAGER NURSERIES
R.F.D. 5, Box 2000
Spotsylvania, VA 22553
List 50 cents
Azaleas and other rhododendrons

HALL RHODODENDRONS
1280 Quince Dr.
Junction City, OR 97448
List $1
Azaleas and other rhododendrons

HASTINGS, H.G., CO.
Box 4274
Atlanta, GA 30302
Old, new, rare, common, ornamental,
edible

HERITAGE ROSARIUM
211 Haviland Mill Rd.
Brookville, MD 20833
List $1
Old roses

HERITAGE ROSE GARDENS
16831 Mitchell Creek Dr.
Fort Bragg, CA 95437
Catalogue $1
Old roses

HIDDEN SPRINGS NURSERY
Rt. 14, Box 159
Cookeville, TN 38501
List $1
Rare fruit trees

HIGH COUNTRY ROSARIUM
1717 Downing St.
Denver, CO 80218
Old roses

HOLBROOK FARM AND NURSERY
P.O. Box 368
Fletcher, NC 28732
Worthy woodies and other select plants

HORTICA GARDENS
Box 308
Placerville, CA 95667
List $1
Conifers

HUDSON, J.L., SEEDSMAN
Box 1058
Redwood City, CA 94064
Catalogue $1
Flowers, nonhybrid vegetables, herbs

HUGHES NURSERY
1305 Wynooche W.
Montesano, WA 98563
List $1.50
Uncommon woodies

JOHNNY'S SELECTED SEEDS
Albion, ME 04910
Edibles

KARTUZ GREENHOUSES
1408 Sunset Dr.
Vista, CA 92083
Catalogue $2
Large collection of begonias, gesneriads,
miniature houseplants, vines, especially
Passiflora

KRISTICK, M. & J.
155 Mockingbird Rd.
Wellsville, PA 17365
Conifers

LAMB NURSERIES, E.
101 Sharp Ave.
Spokane, WA 99202
Outstanding source for perennials

LAMTREE FARM
R.R. 1, Box 162
Warrensville, NC 28693
Uncommon woodies

LAS PILITAS NURSERY
Star Rt. Box 23
Santa Margarita, CA 93453
Catalog $5

LAURAY OF SALISBURY
432 Undermountain Rd.
Rt. 41
Salisbury, CT 06068
Catalogue $2
Cacti, other succulents, orchids, begonias,
gesneriads

LE JARDIN DU GOURMET
Box 98
West Danville, VT 05873
List $1
Outstanding edibles

LE MARCHE SEEDS INTERNATIONAL
Box 190
Dixon, CA 95620
Catalogue $2
Best of edibles from all over

LEUTHARDT, HENRY, NURSERIES
East Moriches, NY 11940
Espalier-trained fruit trees

LIMEROCK ORNAMENTAL GRASSES
R.D. 1, Box 111
Port Matilda, PA 16870
List $1

LOGEE'S GREENHOUSES
141 North St.
Danielson, CT 06239
Catalogue $3
All manner of unusual plants for pots and
gardens, indoors and out

LOUISIANA NURSERY
Rt. 7, Box 43
Opelousas, LA 70570
Catalogue $2
Uncommon woodies

LOWE'S OWN ROOT ROSES
6 Sheffield Rd.
Nashua, NH 03062
Catalogue $2
Old roses

LYON, JOHN D.
143 Alewife Brook Parkway
Cambridge, MA 02140
Bulbs, tubers, corms, rhizomes

MAGNOLIA NURSERY
R.R. 1, Box 43
Chunchula, AL 36521
Uncommon woodies

MCCLURE & ZIMMERMAN
Box 368
Friesland, WI 53935
Bulbs, tubers, corms, rhizomes

MELLINGER'S
2310 W. South Range Rd.
North Lima, OH 44452-9731
All kinds of plants, woody, herbaceous,
ornamental, edible

MERRY GARDENS
Camden, ME 04843
List $1
Herbs, pelargoniums, cultivars of *Hedera
helix*

MILAEGER'S GARDENS
4838 Douglas Ave.
Racine, WI 53402
Catalogue $1
Perennials

MONTROSE NURSERY
Box 957
Hillsborough, NC 27278
List $1.50
Perennials

MOORE MINIATURE ROSES
2529 E. Noble Ave.
Visalia, CA 93277
All kinds of miniature roses, from micro
to moss to hanging basket and tree-form
standard

NATIVE SEEDS/SEARCH
3950 W. New York Dr.
Tucson, AZ 85745
List $1
Seeds of native edibles

NAUMAN, E.B.
688 St. Davids Lane
Schenectady, NY 12309
Conifers

NEW ENGLAND WILDFLOWER SOCIETY
Garden in the Woods
Hemenway Rd.
Framingham, MA 01701
List $2
Wildflowers and ferns

NICHE GARDENS
1111 Dawson Rd.
Chapel Hill, NC 27516
Catalogue $3
Perennials

NICHOLS GARDEN NURSERY
1190 N. Pacific Highway
Albany, OR 97321
Uncommon edibles, flowers, herbs

NOR'EAST MINIATURE ROSES
58 Hammond
Rowley, MA 01969

NORTH CAROLINA STATE UNIVERSITY
ARBORETUM
Box 7609
Raleigh, NC 27695
Membership permits participation in wor-
thy plant propagation and dissemination

NORTHWOODS NURSERY
28696 S. Cramer Rd.
Molalla, OR 97038
Uncommon fruits, nuts, ornamentals

OWENS FARMS
Rt. 3, Box 158A
Ripley, TN 38063
Perennials

PARK, GEO. W., SEED CO.
Greenwood, SC 29647
Something for everyone, new, old, rare,
common

PENSTEMON SOCIETY, AMERICAN
1569 S. Holland Ct.
Lakewood, CO 80226
Annual seed list available to members

PLANTS OF THE SOUTHWEST
1812 Second St.
Santa Fe, NM 87501
Catalogue $2

PORTER & SON
Box 104
Stephensville, TX 76401
Best of old and new vegetables for Southern gardeners

POWELL'S GARDENS
Rt. 3, Box 21
Princeton, NC 27569
Catalogue $2.50
Perennials

ROCKY MOUNTAIN RARE PLANTS
Box 20092
Denver, CO 80220
List $1
Perennials

RONNIGER'S SEED POTATOES
Star Route
Moyie Springs, ID 83845
Catalogue $2
More potatoes than you ever imagined, old, new, from all over the world where the "Irish" potato is grown

ROSES OF YESTERDAY AND TODAY
Brown's Valley Rd.
Watsonville, CA 95076
Catalogue $2
Old roses

ROSLYN NURSERY
211 Burrs Lane
Dix Hills, NY 11746
Catalogue $2
Woodies, perennials

SEEDS BLUM
Idaho City Stage
Boise, ID 83706
Catalogue $2
Heirloom vegetables

SHADY HILL GARDENS
821 Walnut St.
Batavia, IL 60510
Catalogue $2
World's largest collection of geraniums (*Pelargonium*)

SHEPHERD'S GARDEN SEEDS
7389 W. Zayante Rd.
Felton, CA 95018
Catalogue $1
Vegetables, herbs, outstanding descriptions

SHERWOOD GREENHOUSES, J.S. AKIN
Box 6
Sibley, LA 71073
Specialist in pawpaws (*Asimia triloba*)

SKITTONE, ANTHONY J.
1415 Eucalyptus
San Francisco, CA 94132
Catalogue $2
Unusual bulbs, especially from South Africa

SISKIYOU RARE PLANT NURSERY
2825 Cummings Rd.
Medford, OR 97501
Catalogue $2

SONOMA HORTICULTURAL NURSERY
3970 Azalea Ave.
Sebastopol, CA 95472
Catalogue $2
Azaleas and other rhododendrons

SOUTHMEADOW FRUIT GARDENS
15310 Red Arrow Highway
Lakeside, MI 49116

SPINGARN, JOEL W.
Box 782
Georgetown, CT 06829
List $1
Rare conifers, other woodies

STEFFEN, ARTHUR H.
Box 184
Fairport, NY 14450
Clematis

STOKES SEEDS, INC.
Box 548
Buffalo, NY 14240
Large selection of flower, vegetable and herb seeds

STONEHURST RARE PLANTS
1 Stonehurst Court
Pomona, NY 10907
List $1
Conifers

SUNNYBROOK FARMS HOMESTEAD
9448 Mayfield Rd.
Chesterland, OH 44026
Catalogue $1
Perennials, herbs

TAYLOR'S HERB GARDENS
1535 Lone Oak Rd.
Vista, CA 92084
Catalogue $1

TERRAPIN SPRINGS NURSERY
Box 7454
Tifton, GA 31793
List $1
Uncommon woodies

THOMASVILLE NURSERIES
Box 7
Thomasville, GA 31792
Old roses, other woodies, perennials and
edibles

THOMPSON & MORGAN
Box 1308
Jackson, NJ 08527
Rare and common seeds for all kinds of
plants

TOMATO GROWERS SUPPLY CO.
Box 2237
Fort Myers, FL 33902
Nothing but tomatoes

TOMATO SEED CO.
Box 323
Metuchen, NJ 08840
Tomatoes only

TRANS PACIFIC NURSERY
29870 Mill Creek Rd.
Sheridan, OR 97378
Uncommon woodies

TRANSPLANT NURSERY
Parkertown Rd.
Lavonia, GA 30553
Azaleas and other rhododendrons

TWOMBLY NURSERY, INC.
163 Barn Hill Rd.
Monroe, CT
List of woody plants, including *Itea virginica* 'Henry's Garnet,' winner of the pres-
tigious Styer Award

TYTY PLANTATION
Box 159
TyTy, GA 31795
Catalogue $1
Summer bulbs

VAN SCHAIK, MARY MATTISON
Cavendish, VT 05142
List 50 cents
Bulbs

VIETTE, ANDRE, FARM & NURSERY
Rt. 1, Box 16
Fishersville, VA 22939
Catalogue $2
Superb perennials, ornamental grasses

WALKER, MARY, BULB CO.
Box 256
Omega, GA 31775
Bulbs, tubers, corms, rhizomes

WASHINGTON EVERGREEN NURSERY
Box 388
Leicester, NC 28748
Catalogue $2
Conifers

WAVECREST NURSERY
2509 Lakeshore Dr.
Fennville, MI 49408
Uncommon woodies

WAYSIDE GARDENS
One Garden Lane
Hodges, SC 29695-0001
Trees, shrubs, vines, herbaceous peren-
nials, ornamental grasses, bulbs, tubers,
corms, rhizomes

WE-DU NURSERY
Rt. 5, Box 724
Marion, NC 28752
Catalogue $2
Outstanding woody and herbaceous
plants

WELL-SWEEP HERB FARM
317 Mt. Bethel Rd.
Port Murray, NJ 07865
List $1

WHITE FLOWER FARM
Litchfield, CT 06759
Catalogue $5
Woodies, perennials, bulbs

WHITMAN FARMS
1420 Beaumont N.W.
Salem, OR 97304
Woodies, edibles

WINTERTHUR PLANT SHOP
Winterthur, DE 19735
List $1
Uncommon woodies

WOODLANDERS
1128 Colleton Ave.
Aiken, SC 29801
Catalogue $1.50
Worthy woodies; hardy *Passiflora*.

Bibliography

Bailey, L.H. 1928. *The Garden Lover.* New York: The Macmillan Co.

Bailey, Liberty Hyde, and Ethel Zoe Bailey; revised and expanded by the staff of the L.H. Bailey Hortorium. 1976. *Hortus Third.* New York: Macmillan Publishing Co.

Billington, Jill. 1991. *Architectural Foliage.* London: Ward Lock Ltd.

Brickell, Christopher, and Elsley, John. 1989. *The American Horticultural Society Encyclopedia of Garden Plants.* New York: Macmillan Publishing Co.

Christopher, Thomas. 1989. *In Search of Lost Roses.* New York: Summit Books.

Creasy, Rosalind. 1988. *Cooking from the Garden.* San Francisco: Sierra Club Books.

Druse, Ken. 1989. *The Natural Garden.* New York: Clarkson N. Potter, Inc.

Druse, Ken. 1992. *The Natural Shade Garden.* New York: Clarkson N. Potter, Inc.

Elbert, George A. and Virginie F. 1989. *Foliage Plants for Decorating Indoors.* Portland, Oregon: Timber Press.

Glattstein, Judy. 1991. *Garden Design with Foliage.* Pownal, Vermont: Storey Communications, Inc.

Good Housekeeping Editors; Bailey, Ralph; McDonald, Elvin. 1972. *The Goodhousekeeping Illustrated Encyclopedia of Gardening.* New York: Book Division, Hearst Magazines.

Graf, Alfred Byrd. 1974. *Exotic Plant Manual.* East Rutherford, New Jersey: Roehrs Co.

Grounds, Roger. 1990. *Ornamental Grasses.* London: David and Charles.

Guest, C. Z. 1992. *Five Seasons of Gardening.* Boston: Bulfinch Press.

Hampstead, Marilyn. 1984. *The Basil Book.* New York: Long Shadow Books.

Isaacson, Richard T., and the staff of the Andersen Horticultural Library. 1989. *Andersen Horticultural Library's Source List of Plants and Seeds.* Chanhassen, Minnesota: Andersen Horticultural Library, University of Minnesota Libraries, Minnesota Landscape Arboretum.

Krauss, Helen K. 1947. *Begonias for American Homes and Gardens.* New York: Macmillan Publishing Co.

Loewer, Peter. Guest Editor. 1989. *Ornamental Grasses.* Brooklyn, New York: Brooklyn Botanic Garden.

Lovejoy, Ann. 1990. *The Border in Bloom.* Seattle, Washington: Sasquatch Books.

Martin, Tovah. 1991. *The Essence of Paradise: Fragrant Plants for Indoor Gardens.* Boston: Little, Brown and Co.

McDonald, Elvin. 1992. *The New Houseplant: Bringing the Garden Indoors.* New York: Macmillan Publishing Co.

McDonald, Elvin. 1990. *Northeast Gardening.* New York: Macmillan Publishing Co.

Mulligan, William C. 1991. *The Complete Guide to North American Gardens;* Volume 1 Northeast; Volume 2 The West Coast. Boston: Little, Brown and Co.

Sackville-West, Victoria Mary. 1979. *Dearest Andrew: Letters from V. Sackville-West to Andrew Reiber 1951–1952.* New York: Charles Scribner's Sons.

Sedenko, Jerry. 1991. *The Butterfly Garden.* New York: Villard Books.

Simmons, Adelma Grenier. 1964. *Herb Gardening in Five Seasons.* New York: Hawthorn Books, Inc.

Taylor, Kathryn S., and Gregg, Edith W. 1941. *Winter Flowers in Greenhouse and Sun-Heated Pit.* New York: Charles Scribner's Sons.

Wilder, Louise Beebe. 1936; 1990. *Adventures with Hardy Bulbs.* New York: Macmillan Publishing Co. and Collier Books.

Yang, Linda. 1990. *The City Gardener's Handbook from Balcony to Backyard.* New York: Random House.

Index

Page numbers in italic indicate illustrations.

AVERAGE ANNUAL MINIMUM TEMPERATURE

Temperature (°C)	Zone	Temperature (°F)
−45.6 and below	1	below −50
−42.8 to −45.5	2a	−45 to −50
−40.0 to −42.7	2b	−40 to −45
−37.3 to −40.0	3a	−35 to −40
−34.5 to −37.2	3b	−30 to −35
−31.7 to −34.4	4a	−25 to −30
−28.9 to −31.6	4b	−20 to −25
−26.2 to −28.8	5a	−15 to −20
−23.4 to −26.1	5b	−10 to −15
−20.6 to −23.3	6a	−5 to −10
−17.8 to −20.5	6b	0 to −5
−15.0 to −17.7	7a	5 to 0
−12.3 to −15.0	7b	10 to 5
−9.5 to −12.2	8a	15 to 10
−6.7 to −9.4	8b	20 to 15
−3.9 to −6.6	9a	25 to 20
−1.2 to −3.8	9b	30 to 25
1.6 to −1.1	10a	35 to 30
4.4 to 1.7	10b	40 to 35
4.5 and above	11	40 and above

Photo courtesy of the
Agricultural Research Service. U.S.D.A.

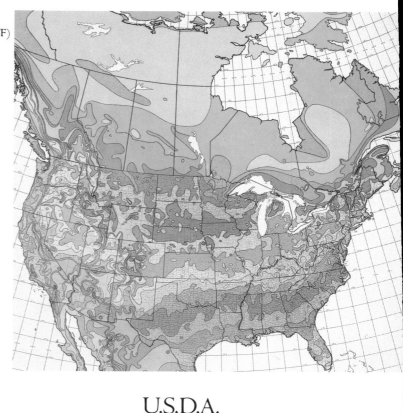

U.S.D.A.
Plant Hardiness
Zone Map